ICONS OF
Opera

ICONS OF
Opera

MATTHEW BOYDEN

THUNDER BAY
P·R·E·S·S

Published in 2001 by
Thunder Bay Press
An imprint of the Advantage Publishers Group
5880 Oberlin Drive, San Diego, CA 92121-4794
www.advantagebooksonline.com

North American edition
Publisher: Ann Ghublikian
Managing Editor: JoAnn Padgett
Project Editor: Elizabeth McNulty

ISBN 1-57145-294-X
Library of Congress Cataloging-in-Publication Data available upon request.

Produced by **Brown Partworks Ltd**
8 Chapel Place, Rivington Street, London EC2A 3DQ, UK
www.brownpartworks.co.uk

Editorial Director: Lindsey Lowe
Project Editor: Dawn Titmus
Design: Wilson Design Associates
Picture Manager: Susannah Jayes
Production Manager: Matt Weyland

Picture Credits
Archive Photos: 84, 96, 98, 100, 102, 112, 118, 132, 140, 166, 168; **Express Newspapers** 70;
Arena Images: 18, 44, 60, 108; **Corbis:** 10, 32, 106; Bettmann 94, 130, 138, 146; **Hulton-
Getty:** 55, 69, 92l, 114, 136, 154, 158, 160; **Lebrecht Collection:** 8, 20, 34, 52, 54, Ilse Buchs
48, R R Gandolfi 12, S Lauterwasser 14, 78, 80, 124, 164, Private Collection 38, 41, 42, 58, 74,
82, 86, 88, 116, 120, 122, 142, Royal Academy of Music 46, 64, 68, 76, 152; Mary Roberts 104;
Scala/Piccagliani 26; Sabine Toepffer 24, 36, 40, 56, 66, 162, 172; Kurt Weill Foundation 90;
Charles B Mintzer: 128, 144, 174; **Performing Arts Library:** 62, 110, 156, 157, Clive Barda
16, 22, 23, 30, 72, Emily Booth 5, 50, Robert Millard 51; **Photostage:** Donald Cooper 148,
150; **Popperfoto:** 134, 170.

Front cover: **Rex Features**; Back cover: **Corbis**; Title page: **Performing Arts Library**.

For Joachim Isaac Vint Boyden,
by way of celebration of his dramatic arrival, stage left.

Printed and bound in Singapore
1 2 3 4 5 01 02 03 04 05

Contents

Introduction

Opera has never been more a part of popular culture than it is today. Nearly every sizable capital city boasts an opera house; recordings of Maria Callas and Luciano Pavarotti can be bought from street stalls in Delhi, Bangkok, and Ulan Bator; pop singers now routinely perform, adapt, and sample operatic arias; and advertising agencies could not survive without recourse to the vast catalog of music and clichés for which opera is internationally celebrated.

Popular myths continue to abound. The image of the corpulent Wagnerian soprano has been exploited to great effect by everyone from Tex Avery to Woody Allen. While such easily exploited stereotypes are founded loosely on fact, it is significant that, for the casual listener as well as the devoted fan, opera has survived as a medium on account of the talent and charisma of its performers, often to the exclusion of the composer. Many believe that our celebrity-led culture is an aberration unique to the 21st century, but during its 400-year history, opera has always been defined by a curious balance of priorities. Indeed, long before fame became an end in itself, rather than a consequence of something more substantial, opera was the world's most fertile source for the production of celebrity.

Since the early 17th century, Europe cultivated a matchless breed of demigod—the singer as superhero. From the outset, the composer was impelled to enter into a demonic pact with his interpreter, and although early composers such as Jacopo Peri frequently sang in productions of their own work, allowing them some control over performances, the skill for writing music was infrequently accompanied by an ability to sing it. At the turn of the 18th century, castrati were the dominant force within the operatic arena. It was for their freakish talents that much of the greatest music of the time was written, and more often than not it was their remarkable skills that filled the theaters. The heroes of the hour, notably Ferri, Siface, Tenducci, and Farinelli, were famed throughout Europe for their extraordinary breath control, their athletic coloratura, and tremendous vocal power, and they were worshiped like gods.

While their vocal talents brought them stature as artists (and their composers' dimly reflected glory), it was singers' personalities, charisma, and egos that helped make opera such a vital and popular entertainment. The current situation, in which Luciano Pavarotti is paid huge sums of money and coddled like royalty, is neither new nor extraordinary. In certain respects, especially when compared to the experience of earlier generations, Pavarotti is grossly underpaid, and he is certainly treated with less reverence than many of the stars who lit up the operatic firmament between 1820 and 1960.

With the exception of all but a handful of composers—chiefly Verdi, Wagner, Puccini, and Richard Strauss—singers have dominated the world of opera to such an extent that even after new music fell from the general culture during the 1930s, stars thrived off the comparative novelty of revivalism—manifest in the bel canto renaissance implemented by Maria Callas and Joan Sutherland and the restoration of early music as a field of quasi-academic study during the 1950s.

With miraculous artists such as Rosa Ponselle, Beniamino Gigli, Titta Ruffo, Renata Tebaldi, Franco Corelli, and Tito Gobbi treading the boards, it was easy to sit back and allow the creative crisis in new music to be eclipsed by the recreative splendor. With the advance of recording technology, the performance and the performers, rather than the work itself, monopolized the vernacular of critics and audiences. The true icons of opera have always been the singers, but today they are alone in sustaining an art form that survives exclusively on a resurrection culture characterized by its repertoire of dead and dying masterworks.

Deciding who warrants inclusion in a book with just 84 spaces has been a very difficult task. The criteria for inclusion have, by necessity, been both highly personal and wildly inconsistent. For example, at least a quarter of the names will be unknown to many readers, since they predate any but the very oldest enthusiast. Francesco Tamagno and Maria Jeritza are included not simply because they were famous during their lifetimes but also because they made a significant and long-lasting impact on the art of singing, dramatic performance, and, to a lesser extent, composition. Other artists, such as Lily Pons and Lisa della Casa, are here because of their defense of a style of singing that was at risk of obsolescence. Many others, notably Ramón Vinay and Giovanni Zenatello, warrant inclusion because of their unique gifts as singers and interpreters. And a number make the grade because of their influence as political animals—chiefly Marian Anderson and Grace Bumbry. The majority are included because of their holistic contribution to operatic culture, as celebrities as well as performers. While every reader will no doubt question the exclusion of a favored artist, no one would question the rights of any of the 84 singers in this book to be considered icons of opera.

The most delicate issue raised by my final selection is the absence of all but a handful of working singers, most of whom are nearing (or in denial of) their retirement. Of fresh talents, there are just four examples. The reason for this is simple: Iconic status among the younger generation requires that a singer is of a caliber so breathtaking that he or she comes to dominate their field many years ahead of their time. For everyone else, such a status comes only with decades of work, and the vast majority of opera's younger names have yet to prove that they have either the staying power or the personality to warrant comparison with the legends in this book. Publicity does not a singer make, and Roberto Alagna, Tito Beltran, José Cura, and Andrea Boccelli may well top the charts, but on current evidence they are never going to find themselves introduced to a hall of fame that includes Enrico Caruso, Giovanni Zenatello, Tito Schipa, Carlo Bergonzi, Franco Corelli, and Luciano Pavarotti.

In the final analysis, this is a highly subjective book, and I hope that both the list of artists and the essays about them will stimulate debate and argument, as well as pleasure.

Pasquale
AMATO
1878 – 1942

ALTHOUGH NOW BEST remembered for his portrayal of Jack Rance at the premiere of Puccini's *La fanciulla del West* in 1910, it was for his performance as Napoleon in the 1928 movie *Glorious Betsy* that Italian baritone Pasquale Amato was commonly known during his lifetime. This hugely popular, Oscar-nominated period romance told of the unlikely love affair between Napoleon's younger brother and an American girl.

In spite of his many fine recordings and legendary first nights, it was thanks to a performance in a silent movie that Amato, one of the 20th century's greatest baritones, achieved his most lasting success. The irony was not lost on Amato, who by 1928 was well past his best. Although he continued to sing into his late fifties, he did so in the tradition of Norma Desmond, living off past glories for want of anything contemporary.

Amato was a child of the *verismo* revolution, and unlike many of those singers called upon to modify their cantabile talents for the new, declamatory style of singing, his breeding and education were molded by the then recently premiered operas by Mascagni, Leoncavallo, and Giordano.

He made his debut in Naples in 1900—the same year as Puccini's *Tosca*—and within three years he was singing in most of the larger European houses, famously at Covent Garden in 1904, where he joined Enrico Caruso in performances of Bizet's *Carmen*. While his repertoire was broad—embracing all the major Verdi roles, as well as Golaud in Debussy's *Pelléas et Mélisande*, Kurwenal in Wagner's *Tristan und Isolde*, and Borodin's Prince Igor—his vibrant, often feverish voice was thought tailor-made to the new music.

As Tonio (Leoncavallo's *Pagliacci*), Marcello (Puccini's *La bohème*), Baron Scarpia (*Tosca*), and Charles Gérard (Giordano's *Andrea Chénier*), he reigned supreme—initially at La Scala and thereafter at the Metropolitan in New York, where from 1908 until 1921 he was the house's leading baritone. This status was assured in 1910, when Puccini chose Amato to join Caruso and Emmy Destinn in the world premiere of *La fanciulla del West*.

Five years later he was asked by Giordano to create the role of Napoleon in his latest opera, *Madame Sans-Gêne*, and in 1908 Puccini asked him to grace the first performance of *Il trittico*. Tragically, he was taken seriously ill shortly before rehearsals and replaced by Giuseppe de Luca. Three years later he was replaced as the Metropolitan's star baritone by Titta Ruffo, from which point can be dated his downfall as a man and an artist.

Returning to Europe, he toured for five years—earning a reputation for vocal unreliability and emotional volatility—before making his way back to the United States, and a career singing for Alfredo Salmaggi's newly formed company at the Hippodrome in New York. Neither his voice, nor his all-consuming despair at its early decline, recovered, and he ended his days as a teacher in New York.

A youthful studio portrait of Amato the handsome baritone, some years before he was immortalized as Napoleon in the movie Glorious Betsy.

Marian
ANDERSON

1 8 9 7 – 1 9 9 3

WHEN IT COMES to determining the iconic status of an opera singer, an evaluation based solely on artistic merit is destined to endless disputation. One of the most visible exceptions to this rule is the American contralto Marian Anderson.

Some 12 months before Jesse Owens dwarfed the Aryan all-comers at the 1936 Berlin Olympics, Anderson was the first black singer to perform at the Salzburg Festival. The Olympics may have attracted a great deal more publicity, but Anderson's achievement was no less significant—not least since she was invited to the festival by a committee monopolized by aspirant Nazis. There can have been no more telling instance of talent overcoming prejudice. Although she is best remembered for having been the first black American to perform at the New York Metropolitan Opera, in 1955, her triumph as a "Negro" in a National Socialist province stands as one of the most resonant in the history of black-American emancipation.

Anderson was born in Philadelphia. She devoted herself to her vocal studies in high school, and when she graduated, the local black community raised enough money for her to travel to New York for lessons with Giuseppe Boghetti. In 1924 she gave her first recital at New York's Town Hall, and the following year she began touring in Europe, giving concerts and studying in England, France, and Germany. While in Salzburg in 1935, she was invited to sing to the archbishop, and her performances attracted the attention of many of Europe's leading musicians. Arturo Toscanini was so moved by her singing that he announced, "Yours is a voice that comes once in a hundred years."

Anderson returned to the United States in 1935 for a recital at New York Town Hall, the success of which brought her to the attention of agent and impresario Sol Hurok. Under his guidance Anderson became the country's third-highest concert box-office draw. But not even her fame could exempt Anderson from racial discrimination, and she was repeatedly turned away from restaurants, hotels, and even concert halls.

Her career became a focus for the civil-rights movement, and there were numerous demonstrations and protests. The most famous incident occurred on April 9, 1939, when the United States Department of the Interior, with the support of First Lady Eleanor Roosevelt, arranged for Anderson to give a concert on the steps of the Lincoln Memorial. The performance attracted a crowd of 75,000 and tens of millions listened on the radio.

On January 7, 1955, she became the first African American to sing on the stage of the Metropolitan. She sang the role of Ulrica in Verdi's *Un ballo in maschera* with rare intensity, winning universal plaudits from her critics. It was a victory of epic proportions—not just for a singer but an entire race—and the length and course of her journey from pauper to icon mirrored the progress of a people reaching out for cultural and social equality.

Anderson appeared on stage in only one role: as Ulrica in Verdi's Un ballo in maschera. *This staged photograph of her "in character" gives a good impression of the power and intensity of her portrayal.*

Cecilia
BARTOLI

b. 1966

CECILIA BARTOLI'S EXTRAORDINARY rise to dominance as the world's foremost Italian mezzo-soprano says much about the famine in talent that has been the hallmark of operatic singing since the 1960s. There is little doubt that Bartoli would have been a star in any age, but that she is now thought to be the only mezzo capable of doing justice to the Italian classical and early romantic repertoire is as typical of the times as it is depressing. Bartoli is a great talent made exceptional by an aggressive marketing apparatus, and it is a wonder that the demands and responsibilities of a premature international career have ruined neither her nor her voice.

Bartoli's parents are both opera singers (in the chorus of Rome Opera), and her mother has remained her only formal voice coach. With their encouragement, she made her debut at the Rome Opera as a nine-year-old in the offstage role of the Shepherd Boy in Puccini's *Tosca*. She turned full time to vocal studies in her 17th year, when it became apparent that she had been born with an entirely natural, unusually mature mezzo-soprano.

Two years later she made her first appearance on television, with the soprano Katia Ricciarelli and the baritone Leo Nucci. The morning after the broadcast, she woke to find herself a national celebrity, and within the month she was being courted by the likes of Daniel Barenboim, Riccardo Muti, Herbert von Karajan, and Decca Records.

Having never performed a complete operatic role, and with little real experience, Bartoli was officially signed in 1988 to Decca Records, which threw vast sums of money into her promotion as the operatic find of the century. Initially, Bartoli restricted herself to recital work, turning only gradually to the theater, but before her 25th birthday, she had made highly publicized stage debuts in Paris (Mozart's *Le nozze di Figaro*), Milan (Rossini's *Le Comte Ory*), Florence (Mozart's *Così fan tutte*), and Barcelona (Rossini's *Il barbiere di Siviglia*).

When not touring, she was in the studio, recording an assortment of roles that she had yet to master on stage. During the 1989/1990 season, for example, she "starred" in recordings of Rossini's *Il barbiere di Siviglia* and *La scala di seta* and Mozart's *Lucio Silla*, *Le nozze di Figaro*, and *Così fan tutte*, which she has since recorded for the second time. As hastily assembled vehicles for the young mezzo, none of these recordings will survive their fevered promotion, but they do highlight the hysteria and impatience of the age.

As the über-mezzo of the 1990s, Bartoli was a circus trick—exploited by a record company that encouraged an appreciation of her performances for all the wrong reasons. A vocal technique is a means, not the end, and it is to be hoped that age will bring with it the wisdom to pace her career and preserve her voice from the ravages of a thrill-seeking, celebrity-starved marketplace.

A typically glamorous portrait of Bartoli, care of her record company, Decca, whose efforts to transform her into an object of desire have been balanced, fortunately, by the natural wonder of her singing.

Kathleen
BATTLE

b. 1948

AS IS OFTEN the case in the media-led world of opera, a performer's many glorious achievements can be obscured by a single, suitably newsworthy indiscretion. American soprano Kathleen Battle's career is a case in point. Until 1994 she was toasted around the world as one of the brightest stars to have emerged during the previous decade, and her performances of the lyric soprano repertoire earned her a reputation second to none for elegance, charm, style, and virtuosity.

These qualities remained conspicuous after 1994, but they were less interesting, and a great deal more common, than her sacking from the New York Metropolitan Opera. Battle's dismissal was a major event—the first high profile termination of a contract at the house since Maria Callas's run-in with Met manager Rudolf Bing.

By all accounts—and there were many—the soprano had begun to believe her own publicity, and although she was commonly adored by the opera-going public, her prima-donna ways were despised by most of those who had to work with her. When news of her dismissal reached the Metropolitan stage, the crew dropped their tools to dance and cheer.

In its defense, the Met accused Battle of "unprofessional actions." Among her more unacceptable habits were her routine absences from rehearsals, her demand that her colleagues leave the stage while she was singing, and that she repeatedly reduced backstage workers to tears. Battle was, and in most respects remains, one of the most talented soubrette sopranos of the postwar generation, but her fall from grace demonstrated that individual talent—unlike company morale—was dispensable.

Her rise to fame as the youngest of seven children of a working-class family was meteoric. She was only 23 when she won her first competition, enabling her to make her debut at the Spoleto Festival in 1972. Less than two years later, she was "discovered" by the conductor James Levine, who chose her to join him in a performance of Mahler's 8th Symphony at the Cincinnati Symphony's 1974 May Festival. Their association lasted 20 years, until Levine, as music director of the New York Metropolitan, was required to endorse her dismissal from the company.

From her Met debut in 1977, as the Shepherd in Wagner's *Tannhäuser*, she triumphed in a repertoire that spanned from Handel to Rossini, Donizetti, and Richard Strauss (*Ariadne auf Naxos*, *Der Rosenkavalier*, and *Arabella*). But because of the size of her voice, it was as a Mozartian soubrette that she was unrivaled, famously as Zerlina (*Don Giovanni*), Despina (*Così fan tutte*), and Pamina (*Die Zauberflöte*).

Though currently lacking a contract with any significant opera company, Battle still earns more than $40,000 a booking, and she has clearly made an effort to mend her ways. Yet for as long as the standoff lasts, the operatic world will remain the poorer for it.

Soft-focus photography and high styling emphasize the air of manufactured celebrity that characterized Battle's rise to stardom. This photograph gives little hint of how sudden would be her fall.

Carlo
BERGONZI

b. 1924

AS A RULE, tenors who successfully win the affection of the gallery rarely have the same good fortune with the critics. Alone in satisfying both quarters was Italian Carlo Bergonzi, the foremost tenor stylist of postwar opera and one of the finest musicians ever to grace the tenor register.

Where his peers relied on technique to see them physically through a performance, Bergonzi demonstrated how a vocal method might be used to appease the composer as well as the crowd. Uniquely among postwar tenors, he brought a voice of great size, flexibility, and warmth to a section of repertoire that was more often than not the province of shouters. It is true that his remarkable expressive range evolved by way of necessity, since he was one of the least proficient actors in operatic history. Yet such was the emotion inspired by this irreplaceable artist that at his British farewell to Covent Garden in 1991, half the audience spent two-thirds of the evening in tears.

Like many other tenors of the 1950s and 1960s, Bergonzi began his operatic career as a baritone. His studies were interrupted by World War II, and not until 1948 was he able to make his official debut, as Rossini's Figaro, in Lecce. Two years later, having discovered by chance that he was able to reach a high C, he moved up a register, retraining as a tenor, and in 1951 he made his second debut, as Giordano's Andrea Chénier. That same year he played a major role in the national broadcast celebrations to commemorate the anniversary of Verdi's death, and in 1953 he sang for the first time at La Scala. Five years later he was signed by Decca Records. Thereafter, Bergonzi featured on some of the finest opera recordings ever made, including outstanding productions of *La bohème* (Puccini, 1958), *Madama Butterfly* (Puccini, 1958), *Aida* (Verdi, 1959), *Un ballo in maschera* (Verdi, 1961), *La traviata* (Verdi, 1962), and *Don Carlos* (Verdi, 1965).

During these halcyon years (1958–1965), when Bergonzi was in his prime, there was no one to touch him as a Verdi tenor. He demonstrated an instinctive feel for Verdian style, judging perfectly the composer's uneven phrase lengths and expressive disciplines. As Nemorino (Donizetti's *L'elisir d'amore*), Alvaro (Verdi's *La forza del destino*), Edgardo (Verdi's *Lucia di Lammermoor*), and Simon Boccanegra (Verdi), he was without rival.

Toward the end of the 1960s and during the 1970s, Bergonzi's choices in repertoire, compounded by a heavy workload, diluted the firm vibrato and steady tone that characterized his earlier work. Although he could still place his voice better than any other tenor of his generation, by 1975 he was a shadow of his former self. Despite a series of moving farewells during the 1990s, he has continued to sing, and while these excursions have done his reputation no favors, it will take a great deal more than vanity to tarnish his standing as arguably the 20th century's most gifted and thoughtful Italian tenor.

This photograph of Bergonzi as Manrico in Verdi's Il trovatore *at Covent Garden in 1978 captures perfectly the singer's placing of the voice, just as it does his infamous artlessness as an actor.*

Jussi
BJÖRLING

1 9 1 1 – 1 9 6 0

IT IS SADLY often the case that those blessed with the greatest talent are also those least able to deal with it. Swedish tenor Jussi Björling—thought by many to be the finest lyric tenor of the 20th century—was to most of the world a humble, quietly spoken man. To those who knew him he was, in the words of his accompanist Ivor Newton, "obstinate, difficult, taciturn, and unusually lazy." Beset by nerves, crippled by self-doubt, and, for most of his adult life, awash with alcohol, he lived a life defined by anguish.

Born with a voice of almost limitless flexibility and richness, Björling responded unusually badly to the pressures of public life and the expectations of unforgiving audiences. It is a testament to his remarkable abilities that he was able to enjoy such a winning career despite the many demons that made him such an unhappy colleague.

Björling studied with his father as a child, making his public debut at the age of five as part of the Björling Male Quartet, which toured throughout Scandinavia and the United States for 10 years to popular acclaim. When it was apparent that his magnificent treble was maturing into an equally glorious tenor, he was sent to John Forsell at the Royal Academy of Music in Stockholm, who prepared him for his operatic debut in 1930 at the Royal Swedish Opera. Within four years Björling had performed an extraordinary 44 roles throughout Europe, had made dozens of recordings for HMV, and had been invited to make his American debut.

The trajectory of his career in the United States was all the more astonishing because Björling was not Italian. At a time when Italian tenors prevailed, it was difficult, and frequently impossible, for non-Italians to break into the standard repertory. But Björling was practically dragged into the Metropolitan, where he made his debut as Rodolfo (Puccini's *La bohème*) in 1937. Thereafter, he sang a wide variety of roles, later specializing in the romantic French and Italian repertoire.

Like his character, Björling's tenor was melancholy and lachrymose, and the exceptional range, power, and warmth could never dispel the overriding sense of a voice "heavy with unshed tears." Even in the most exhilarating music there was a sense that deep down the singer was attempting to convey emotions of which he was himself unaware.

While the continued popularity of his recordings attest to his status as one of the most cherished singers of the 20th century, there are many who feel that the instrument came too effortlessly to the singer. On most of his complete recordings there is a dearth of interpretive variety and an absence of expressive character for which no amount of vocal pyrotechnics can ever truly compensate. Björling was clearly one of the most naturally gifted singers in operatic history, but his life and career would seem to bear out the axiom that true greatness never comes easily.

Before he was overtaken by alcoholism, Björling was a handsome man as well as a peerless singer. This early portrait of him shows him in costume as the Duke of Mantua in Verdi's Rigoletto.

Inge
BORKH

b. 1921

ICONS NEED NOT be famous to be iconic; neither is it necessary for them to have worked their way onto the pedestal of achievement—icons need only to have influenced the understanding of their province. While even keen opera-goers may never have heard of, or listened to, the German-born Swiss dramatic soprano Inge Borkh, her influence continues to filter through to posterity, and she remains one of the most significant German singers of the 20th century.

Born in Mannheim, Germany, into a theatrical family, she pursued an acting career, appearing as a student at the Burgtheater in Mannheim, before turning to singing in her late teens. She made her debut in Lucerne, Switzerland, in 1941, but continued to study and practice for another decade until, aged 30, she took her first major role in 1951—as Magda in the German-language premiere of Menotti's *The Consul*. She was then snapped up by the Bavarian State Opera, from where she regularly traveled throughout Europe and the United States, performing a small repertoire of roles. Two, in particular, made her famous: Richard Strauss's Elektra in 1953 and Verdi's Lady Macbeth in 1955.

Thanks to a combination of theatrical instinct, incisive declamation, dramatic concision, and musical intelligence, she brought to her performances a poetical clarity that had, for years, been lost to the fashion of beauty for beauty's sake. Even during his lifetime, Strauss lamented the failure of singers to animate his characters through the detail and gravity of his poet's verses.

Great singing on its own—as epitomized, for example, by the work of Birgit Nilsson—impresses for its own sake, but Borkh placed her no less thrilling voice at the service of the poet first and the composer second. Her tragically few recordings pay tribute to this remarkable gift, but it is as Elektra, in a 1960 recording conducted by Karl Böhm, that her genius for music theater is most fully demonstrated. The mesmeric intensity of the singing alone is enough to warrant the most fulsome of eulogies, but Borkh's portrayal of Elektra's mental decay and emotional release through her complete identification with Hugo von Hofmannsthal's poetry makes her performance, and the production as a whole, a revelation.

Borkh was even capable of bringing a human frailty to the monstrous figure of Turandot (Puccini), and her Salome (Strauss) remains one of the few portrayals to have satisfied the composer's prescription for a "16-year-old Isolde." The remarkable expressivity of her performances and the hypnotic intensity of her complete immersion into the few roles she accepted may have escaped the popular consciousness, but like no other postwar soprano, she managed to bring to her repertoire a clarity and an intensity that continue to represent the ideal.

Borkh was not a conventionally beautiful woman, but her strong features suited her portrayal of strong women, most famously Elektra, Salome, Lady Macbeth, and, as in this photograph, Isolde.

Grace
BUMBRY

b. 1937

IN THE WAKE of Marian Anderson's pioneering achievements as a black American singer, the most capable ambassador for color blindness in opera was the American mezzo-soprano Grace Bumbry. At a time when an appearance by a black artist in any of the world's major opera houses was still something of an event, Bumbry made history in 1961 when, at the invitation of Wieland Wagner, she became the first black singer to appear on stage at the Bayreuth Festival.

Although there was an air of media manipulation about the whole event, it still took enormous courage for Bumbry to walk, eyes open, into the lion's den. She was engaged to sing the part of Venus (Wagner's *Tannhäuser*), and from the outset she was daily made aware of her "unsuitability" to the role by a number of her festival associates. Many of the more hardline critics attacked the "Black Venus" as an aberration, and, for all Wieland's pleading, Bumbry never returned to the scene of her most visible triumph.

ABOVE: Bumbry was one of the few African-Americans to succeed as an opera singer—most famously at the Bayreuth Festival in 1961.

Outside the rarefied atmosphere of Bayreuth, Bumbry was hailed as one of the finest mezzo-sopranos of her generation. After studying with Lotte Lehmann between 1955 and 1958, Bumbry was joint winner of the 1958 Metropolitan Auditions, a triumph that assured her a prosperous American career. Instead, however, she chose to travel to Europe and had a hugely successful Parisian debut in 1960 as Amneris (Verdi's *Aida*). The same year she joined Basle Opera, from where word quickly spread of Bumbry's exquisite voice and expressive talents. She was engaged by Covent Garden in 1963 and the New York Metropolitan in 1965. Her American career was long and glorious, but it was for her work in Europe that she is best remembered.

Bumbry revealed an exceptional flair for physical and vocal characterization, as well as a rare capacity for dividing her voice between mezzo and soprano roles. In the light of her status as a black woman in a "white man's world," it is fitting that she should have appeared on a number of the finest opera recordings of the 20th century (where only her singing talents count for merit), and that arguably the best of them should be an electrifying rendition of her celebrated performance at Bayreuth as the "Black Venus."

OPPOSITE: Covent Garden's 1977 production of Salome, *starring Bumbry, was famous for the excess of its costumes as well as for the performances of its leading lady.*

Montserrat
CABALLÉ

b. 1933

THE SPANISH SOPRANO Montserrat Caballé made two lasting contributions to operatic culture. The first was her development of the dramatic bel canto method that, thanks largely to her efforts, returned to broad popularity during the 1960s. The second was her validation of the saying that an opera was only truly over when the fat lady had sung. Although her girth grew steadily more generous with time, her proportions had little bearing on the beauty, subtlety, and power of her voice.

Although Caballé was incapable of the displays of virtuosity associated with Maria Callas or Joan Sutherland, hers was by some way the more beautiful instrument. She was careful to choose roles that suited her, and was unrivaled in the dramatic bel canto roles of Donizetti and Verdi, establishing a near-monopoly over Donizetti's regal heroines— namely Elizabeth I (*Roberto Devereux*), Maria Stuarda, and Anna Bolena.

Having studied for over a decade at the Barcelona Liceo, Caballé won the college's Gold Medal in 1954. Two years later she was immediately employed by Basle Opera, where she mastered a broad compass of roles, including everything from Pamina (Mozart's *Die Zauberflöte*), Aida (Verdi), and Tosca (Puccini) to Richard Strauss's Arabella, Chrysothemis (*Elektra*), and Salome.

From Basle she toured throughout Europe and on April 20, 1965, she replaced an indisposed Marilyn Horne in a New York concert performance of *Lucrezia Borgia* (Donizetti). Such was her success that Caballé found herself transformed overnight from a "jack-of-all-trades" soprano into a bel canto specialist. Impresarios competed to unearth lost and forgotten scores by Donizetti as vehicles for her talents, and during the ensuing decade she prevailed as the world's leading dramatic bel canto soprano.

At her peak Caballé's voice was uniquely beautiful, and she used it with memorable taste and discretion. Her technique was such that she could spin the endless legato phrases required by Donizetti's music without effort, and she could float at the top of the soprano register like no other. Although she lacked Callas's fire-and-brimstone theatricality, she never resorted to the note-spinning of Sutherland. Somewhere between the two she was, perhaps, the embodiment of the best of both worlds.

By the early 1980s Caballé's voice was on the wane, and in an act of questionable artistic merit, she joined Freddie Mercury, the lead singer of the pop group Queen, in a series of singles that reached its popular zenith in 1987 with the release of the mock-operatic "Barcelona." Caballé continued to perform in the opera house until the 1990s, when it was generally agreed that she was some way past her best. An immense woman of corresponding charm and warmth, Caballé has devoted her career since to teaching, fund-raising, and concert work.

Caballé was one of the best-loved stars of the postwar generation, gifted with extraordinary talents, a generous personality, and a physical presence to match.

Maria
CALLAS

1 9 2 3 – 1 9 7 7

UNTIL RECENTLY THE world of opera has proved necessarily tolerant of personality disorders—necessarily, since the careers of divas such as Francesca Cuzzoni, Faustina Bordoni, Adelina Patti, Nellie Melba, and Luisa Tetrazzini have repeatedly demonstrated that true genius is rarely obliging, and never prosaic. Perhaps the most famous diva of them all, and arguably the most complete opera soprano of the 20th century, was American, later Greek, soprano Maria Callas.

Not only was she the finest singing actress of her generation, but for most of her professional career she was the supreme embodiment of opera chic. She endured an international celebrity that, in modern times, can be compared only to that of Luciano Pavarotti. She possessed a beauty idolized by the finest designers and photographers, and she was courted by the world's most eligible bachelors, eventually marrying the most eligible of them all, Aristotle Onassis.

At the start of her career, Callas sang almost everything asked of her. Between 1941, when she made her official debut as Tosca (Puccini), and 1947, when she worked for the first time with the conductor Tullio Serafin, Callas was a dramatic soprano whose roles included Aida (Verdi), Turandot (Puccini), Isolde (Wagner's *Tristan und Isolde*), Kundry (Wagner's *Parsifal*), Leonore (Beethoven's *Fidelio*), and Brünnhilde (Wagner's *Der Ring*).

In 1949 she stepped in at the last minute to cover for an indisposed colleague in a performance of the florid role of Elvira in *I Puritani* (Bellini). Her performance was such that, with Serafin's guidance, it led to her reinvention as a coloratura soprano, and over the following decade she did more than any other singer to revive the bel canto tradition.

As Norma (Bellini), Médée (Cherubini), Anna Bolena (Donizetti), Lucia (Donizetti's *Lucia di Lammermoor*), Lady Macbeth (Verdi's *Macbeth*), Violetta (Verdi's *La traviata*), and Tosca (Puccini), Callas was, and remains, without rival. It was not that the voice was in any traditional sense beautiful—indeed, from as early as 1954, the opposite would be true—rather it was the intensity with which she used it that made every performance such an absorbing theatrical event. No other soprano demonstrated such instinctive dramatic intuition, and she was unique in being able to turn the least substantial role into a living, breathing, sympathetic individual.

Throughout the 1950s, when she recorded extensively for EMI, Callas's voice deteriorated steadily, and when she came to make her last operatic performance, on July 5, 1965 (as Tosca at Covent Garden), it was clear that, like Tosca, she, too, had suffered for her art. The famous Callas temper, and the intense jealousy and impatience that typified her working habits (leading to her famous dismissal from the New York Metropolitan), can be ascribed to this traumatic decline.

One of the biggest stars ever to grace an opera stage, Callas was also one of its most beautiful. Here she appears as Violetta—a Parisian society hostess of the 1850s suffering from consumption—in Verdi's La traviata.

Emma
CALVÉ

1 8 5 8 – 1 9 4 2

On May 30, 1894, British dramatist and critic George Bernard Shaw wrote of a performance by French soprano Emma Calvé as Bizet's Carmen that it "shocked me beyond measure…Her Carmen is a superstitious, pleasure-loving good-for-nothing, caught by the outside of anything glittering, with no power but the power of seduction, which she exercises without sense or decency…Her death scene, too, is horribly real…to see Calvé finally tumble down a mere heap of carrion, is to get much the same sensation as might be given by the reality of a brutal murder." For modern readers, Shaw's depiction of Calvé's portrayal of Carmen may seem like a representative interpretation of the character's sexually manipulative personality. However, at the end of the 19th century, such a wanton subscription to the pleasure principle was audaciously risqué. Calvé's blatant physical self-awareness, unabashed sexual confidence, and heightened dramatic sensibilities, consolidated by a voice of compelling flair and adaptability, ideally equipped her to become the first soprano to shake the cobwebs of probity from what had, until then, been an opera in suspended animation. Thanks to Calvé, Carmen finally came to life.

Calvé's career as the operatic seductress par excellence began in 1890, nearly a decade after her debut, in 1881, in Brussels as Marguerite in Gounod's *Faust*. She was on her second visit to La Scala, Milan, and after appearing as Ophélie in Thomas's *Hamlet*, she was catapulted to celebrity and a run of performances as Santuzza in Mascagni's *Cavalleria rusticana*. As the latter she so impressed Mascagni that he invited her to Rome to create the role of Suzel in the first production of his latest opera, *L'amico Fritz*. Thereafter she was a favorite in London and New York, where her performances as Santuzza and especially Carmen transformed her into a living legend.

She was much admired by numerous other composers, including Puccini, Richard Strauss, and Massenet, who wrote two operas for her: *Sapho* and *La navarraise*. Her voice, which spanned both soprano and mezzo registers, was remarkable for its warmth, power, and extension—originally reaching a high F, the technique for which she claimed to have learned from the Italian castrato Domenico Mustafà.

Most importantly, Calvé was a superb actress (thanks, in part, to the advice and assistance of French baritone Victor Maurel) with a capricious spontaneity all her own, and it was this extravagant, improvisatory charisma that made her one of the most compelling performers of the 19th century. The British pianist Ivor Newton, who accompanied her on numerous occasions, believed that as far as Calvé was concerned, "music was only a vehicle for her own remarkably attractive personality, not an art to which she could dedicate herself." In truth, Calvé was an extremely hardworking and attentive musician, but her enthusiasm did frequently get the better of her.

Calvé was celebrated for the sexual excess of her portrayal of Bizet's Carmen, but no photograph could ever quite capture the energy and eroticism of her performances. She was also famed for her mastery of the tambourine.

José
CARRERAS

b. 1946

DURING THE DECADE starting from his official debut in Barcelona in 1970—as Flavio in Bellini's *Norma*—Spaniard José Carreras was without rival as the world's most naturally gifted, musically intelligent lyric tenor. In most respects, he stands comparison with the greatest of the century, Enrico Caruso included. For the extraordinary beauty and energy of his singing and for the irresistible sense of style that characterized his finest work, his career ranks as one of the most precious, if tragically brief, in the history of opera.

Struggles with adversity always make for great copy, and the public's response to Carreras's widely publicized battle with leukemia in 1986 demonstrated the depth of public affection for him. But if Carreras successfully conquered his illness, then his return to public performance in 1988, moving as it was, confirmed that while the battle to save the singer had been won, the battle to save the voice had been lost. Of course, the process of decline was due only in part to cancer—the primary cause was a series of spectacularly poor choices in repertoire that placed his flawless, but specialized, talents under terminal stress.

Carreras's talents were manifest even before his voice broke. Recordings of him as a child, including one famous performance of "La donna è mobile," confirmed the existence of a formidable talent, and after studying piano, he began formal singing lessons in 1963. He was "discovered" by Montserrat Caballé, who took him under her considerable wing, urging theaters to engage them together as a package. Before long Carreras was in demand all over the world, particularly in the United States, where, for his performances as Oronte (Verdi's *I Lombardi*), the Duke (Verdi's *Rigoletto*), and Alfredo (Verdi's *La traviata*), he was hailed as Carlo Bergonzi's natural successor in the lyric repertoire.

He soon began making recordings, some of which—Edgardo (Donizetti's *Lucia di Lammermoor*, 1976), the Italian Singer (Richard Strauss' *Der Rosenkavalier*, 1976), Cavaradossi (Puccini's *Tosca*, 1976), and Don Carlos (Verdi, 1977)—rank among the finest ever made. During these halcyon days, the voice was remarkably secure, with an infectiously warm middle register, great power, and a seductive turn of phrase, achieved partly through his expressive use of portamento and vibrato.

Unfortunately, Carreras suffered from "Di Stefano syndrome," whereby a naturally lyric tenor decides to sing roles outside his natural range. Toward the end of the 1970s, he began to tackle much heavier repertoire—including Radamès (Verdi's *Aida*), Calaf (Puccini's *Turandot*), and Andrea Chénier (Giordano)—which led him to force his voice to unnatural extremes. Carreras's singing since the 1980s, including his dismal performances as one third of the Three Tenors, has obscured the truth of his talent—that he was by some way the most gifted of them all. While he continues to sing even now, his career is living proof that the candle that burns brightest also burns fastest.

In his prime Carreras was the greatest of the Three Tenors, with an intense stage presence to match the wondrous richness and vitality of his voice. He was never better than as Don José in Bizet's Carmen, *as whom he is seen here.*

Enrico
CARUSO

1 8 7 3 – 1 9 2 1

IN 1897, HAVING recently performed the role of Rodolfo in Puccini's latest opera, *La bohème*, the Italian tenor Enrico Caruso visited the composer at his villa for an audition. He had sung less than a page of music when Puccini leaped from the piano and exclaimed "Who sent you to me—God?" He was not alone in thinking Caruso divine. Since making his first recordings in 1900, the name Caruso has been synonymous with vocal perfection.

More than a century since his debut, in 1895, Caruso is still the tenor's tenor, the exception to every established rule and the embodiment of operatic excellence. He is the trinity of Italian *tenorismo*, and he remains the 20th century's only male opera singer to have prevailed, alive and dead, outside the normal parameters of criticism.

Even at the beginning of his career, when by his own admission he lacked technique, the basic quality of the voice was like no other. The warmth, effortless breath control, and uncommon power set him apart from even the most talented of his peers. Thanks partly to the *verismo* culture in which he worked, he developed a stylistic security that enabled him to bridge both the new style of high dramatic declamation as well as the old romantic style of floated bel canto. His versatility enabled him to sing Nemorino (Donizetti's *L'elisir d'amore*) on one night and Canio (Leoncavallo's *Pagliacci*) the next, modifying his approach to the differing styles of music and character without compromising either.

Having made his debut at the height of the Italian operatic renaissance, Caruso was very much part of the new music scene. Between 1894 and 1902 he sang in the premieres of nearly a dozen new operas, including *Fedora* (Giordano), *Iris* (Mascagni), and *L'arlesiana* (Cilea). But once he began making records, and with his move in 1902 to the United States, Caruso proved himself capable of singing almost anything. He was as popular in the lyric French repertoire as he was in the standard Italian repertoire on which his reputation was founded.

After making his debut at the New York Metropolitan in 1902, he enjoyed an uninterrupted career as the most popular musician in American history. Of his 57 roles and 832 career performances, 37 of those roles and 607 of the performances were given at the Metropolitan. Although the famous aphorism "The gramophone made Caruso, and Caruso made the gramophone" is fair up to a point, there is no question that, had he never made a single record, he would still have prevailed on reputation alone as the finest tenor of the 20th century. The voice was enormous, uncommonly baritonal, but never vulgar or ugly. He could be fiery and impulsive, but it was the remarkable, unique warmth of the instrument to which no other tenor has come even close. Caruso's brilliant career was cut short by pleurisy at the age of 47. He gave his last public performance at the Metropolitan on Christmas Eve, 1920, and died in Naples in August 1921.

Caruso as he appeared while singing the clown's tragic aria "Vesti la giubba" from Leoncavallo's Pagliacci. *This was, perhaps, Caruso's most popular role.*

Fyodor
CHALIAPIN

1873–1938

IN 1926 THE British critic Ernest Newman noted perceptively of the Russian bass Fyodor Chaliapin that he was "among all singers the one most in need of being seen in order to be properly heard." Uniquely among 20th-century opera stars, Chaliapin's success and cumulative influence as an opera singer existed independently of his singing. Where, for example, the artistry of Beniamino Gigli was exclusively vocal, Chaliapin was first and foremost a dramatist. By his own admission his qualities were, in order of priority, "as an actor and a singer."

Indeed, had posterity judged Chaliapin's achievements through his recordings alone, then his reputation might be a great deal less distinguished. Recordings of opera stars have always thrown a pale shadow of their subject, but Chaliapin's art was so completely defined by his physical presence that, with one or two exceptions, even his finest work in the studio conveys little of the demonic, mesmerizing vitality of his work in the opera house. According to Russian producer Konstantin Stanislavsky, "Synthesis has rarely been achieved by anyone in the arts, particularly in the theater. Chaliapin is the only case I can think of. My system is taken straight from Chaliapin."

Chaliapin was born into poverty in Kazan. After six years as a choirboy, he discovered the theater. As he later recalled, the theater "drove me out of my mind, made me almost beside myself…I was totally committed to my vocation. I had no other ruling passion whatever, no particular taste for anything other than the stage." Necessarily, it took him many years—and the relentless instruction of Tchaikovsky's friend Dmitry Usatov— before he found his voice. Once found, he devoted it to the isolation "of the character behind the music." Having realized that "in the color of the word and phrase lies all the strength of singing," he was able to bring a role to life on stage.

The famous "Chaliapin metamorphosis" was brought to bear on an enormous number of roles, but his most celebrated were the Mephistopheles of Gounod and Boito—the latter, on seeing Chaliapin as his Mephistopheles, exclaimed, "At last I see my own conception of the role! At last I have found my devil"—Massenet's Don Quichotte, Borodin's Prince Igor, and Mussorgsky's Boris Godounov.

His huge frame, elastic features, and genius for makeup contributed to his almost superhuman charisma, but it was his harmonization of talents that made him one of the miracles of operatic theater. Lotte Lehmann appeared once with Chaliapin: "The impression he made was indescribable…a tall figure appeared above me that twisted its way along the window like some frightful spider…An indefinable terror made me go cold. This was no longer opera, this had turned into some terrible reality. And when the curtain came down, and Mephistopheles changed back into Chaliapin, I breathed a sigh of relief."

Chaliapin is thought by many to have been the greatest stage actor of his, or any, generation. Here he is seen in typically intimidating form as Ivan the Terrible.

Boris
CHRISTOFF

1914–1993

THE SHADOW THROWN by Fyodor Chaliapin was considerable. Even the very greatest talents have had to compete with his legacy as the finest bass-singing actor of the 20th century. One of the few to have broken free of this suffocating birthright was Bulgarian bass Boris Christoff. An actor of outstanding intensity, Christoff was closely associated throughout his long career with many of the same Russian singing-acting roles mastered by Chaliapin, but where Chaliapin was limited as a singer, Christoff's uniquely flexible and fluent voice entitled him to perform operas outside the Russian canon.

Born in Plovdiv, Bulgaria, he studied law before becoming a member of the celebrated Gusla Choir. As a member of the choir, he was discovered by King Boris of Bulgaria, who supported Christoff's move in 1941 to Italy and a period of study with the Italian baritone Riccardo Stracciari.

Christoff finally made his debut, as Colline in *La bohème* (Puccini), in 1946, and 12 months later he was heard for the first time as Pimen in *Boris Godounov* (Mussorgsky) at both La Scala and Rome Opera. It was obvious to everyone that Christoff was poorly cast, and two years later, in 1949, he made his debut as Boris (*Boris Godounov*) in London. The critical response confirmed the emergence of a truly great artist in the Chaliapin mold, but with the added luxury of a perfectly placed, highly malleable, and beautiful bass voice.

His reputation as a "Russian" bass took him round the world, but he quickly dispelled the assumption that he would limit himself to the Cyrillic repertoire. As audiences discovered during the 1950s, Christoff was equally at home in the French, Italian, and German repertoires, excelling as Giulio Cesare (Handel), Rocco (Beethoven's *Fidelio*), King Marke (Wagner's *Tristan und Isolde*), Hagen (Wagner's *Der Ring*), and Gurnemanz (Wagner's *Parsifal*). If Christoff's Wagner hailed from east of the Urals (he was never invited to Bayreuth), then his performances as the Mephistopheles of Gounod and Boito and as King Philip II of Spain (Verdi's *Don Carlos*) cemented Christoff's reputation as the greatest operatic bass of his generation.

Like Chaliapin's, part of Christoff's charm was his exaggerated approach to acting, but the eye-rolling, face-pulling, and overheated characterizations suited his choice of roles, and unlike most of his peers, he was able to inject huge significance into every word and phrase. If he was often accused of overplaying his hand dramatically, then few ever questioned the hypnotic beauty of his singing or his personal magnetism.

Christoff's work on record captures memorably his great appeal as a singing actor, at the same time confirming the unique quality of one of the 20th century's most lyrical and versatile bass voices.

Unlike Fyodor Chaliapin, who was limited outside the Russian repertoire, Christoff was a master of French, German, and Italian opera—most famously as Gounod's Faust and as King Philip II of Spain in Verdi's Don Carlos, *as seen here in this photograph of him at the Bavarian State Opera in 1977.*

Franco
CORELLI

b. 1921

THE ITALIAN TENOR Franco Corelli was to the opera-going audiences of the 1950s and 1960s what Mario Lanza was to everyone else. In most respects, he remains the ideal of the operatic tenor—as beautiful to look upon as to listen to, but tortured by a rack of psychological insecurities that made him quite as tragic a figure as Lanza. Corelli's misfortune was to have been born with probably the most viscerally impressive tenor voice of the 20th century, a curse quite as disabling as Lanza's hedonism. Perpetually dissatisfied with his work, he suffered from a crippling lack of personal satisfaction.

He pushed himself to extraordinary lengths, living a life of almost monastic self-discipline, and his career was defined by a relentless process of study, self-criticism, and technical refinement. This ritual enabled him to take his unnaturally dark tenor and modify it to tackle some of the most difficult, high-reaching bel canto roles in opera, but it also led to a reputation for preciousness, unreliability, and narcissism.

This reputation was accurate only in that he might simply not show up to a performance if he felt uncertain of the outcome, but such was his pulling power with audiences, and so exciting was he to work with, that few ever raised an objection. If he was a little eccentric—he would frequently refuse to perform unless he received his increasingly vast fees in cash, on occasions hurriedly stuffed into carrier bags—then his unorthodox attitude to his responsibilities as an artist, and the expectations of his audiences, conspired to produce some of the greatest performances ever seen on an operatic stage.

Nicknamed "Golden Thighs" by the chorus at the Met in New York, Corelli stood at six foot two (1.88 m) without shoes, and had the sort of looks and physique that film stars dream about. Yet none of his colleagues begrudged him his advantages since most were simply too grateful to be standing next to him in the first place. On stage, sopranos were known to faint during duets, chorus members would forget what they were supposed to be doing, and orchestral players would remain after performances to add their applause to the adulation of the audience.

In the end Corelli was a Faustian creature, a man gifted beyond measure but doomed never to enjoy his gifts. His recordings give some idea of the animal excitement he generated, just as they convey the teeth-rattling high notes and breath-defying phrasing. He was no stylist, and his swooping, aspirate diction had many critics, but in the roles that he made his own—Andrea Chénier (Giordano), Manrico (Verdi's *Il trovatore*), Canio (Leoncavallo's *Pagliacci*), Don Alvaro (Verdi's *La forza del destino*), Radamès (Verdi's *Aida*), Werther (Massenet), and Don José (Bizet's *Carmen*)—he was simply unrivaled. As the mezzo-soprano Grace Bumbry recalled: "I wish you could have seen Corelli just once on the stage. When they say class, that was class. When they say voice, that was *the* voice."

A typically flattering studio portrait of probably the most handsome tenor of the 20th century. Corelli's electrifying performances invariably lived up to his appearance, for which he was known at the Met as "Golden Thighs."

Lisa
DELLA CASA

b. 1919

ARGUABLY THE LAST great stylist of the Viennese school, and certainly one of the 20th century's most seductive talents, was Swiss soprano Lisa della Casa. Before the advent of recording, different regions and individual cities fostered their own, singular approach to vocal style and effect. By the end of the 1960s, however, the kaleidoscopic variety of expression gave way to a generic stylization that turned difference into eccentricity. Della Casa's talents rested with the music of two composers, Mozart and Richard Strauss—both of them central to the early 20th-century Austrian vocal tradition of which she was such a peerless example.

Della Casa's was a soprano of extraordinary beauty, intimacy, passion, and eroticism—a voice of unique capabilities that, for all its expressive substance, was wholly defined by the culture that formed it. The inimitable phrasing, liberal use of portamento, prevalent head tones, extended legatos, and unusual, aspiritic diction were not to everyone's tastes. But in the 1940s such qualities allied della Casa to the lyric Viennese tradition so popular before World War II. She was vocally and temperamentally predisposed to the heavy stylization of the Viennese school, and her earliest recordings, from the 1940s, prove that the unmistakable mannerisms of her maturity were cultivated, rather than instinctive.

ABOVE: Della Casa was famed for her unique appearance—elegant and beautiful—as well as for the brilliance of her voice.

In 1947 she appeared for the first time at the Salzburg Festival, as Zdenka (Strauss's *Arabella*). The same year she joined the Vienna State Opera. She returned to Salzburg in 1948, as Madeleine in *Capriccio* (Strauss), and in 1951 she performed for the first time at Glyndebourne, where she sang the Countess in *Le nozze di Figaro* (Mozart). In 1953 she made her debut at the New York Metropolitan.

In the Strauss repertoire she was one of the few sopranos of her generation to sing all three of *Der Rosenkavalier*'s leads. She was a virile, if somewhat refined, Salome, a wonderfully fragile Chrysothemis (*Elektra*), and a deliciously complex Ariadne (*auf Naxos*). But it was as Arabella that della Casa shone at her brightest. Her charm, class, and physical beauty were perfectly tailored to the role. Although a memorable actress, it is the voice—arguably the most beautiful German soprano since Lotte Lehmann's—that remains, and it reminds us that provincial traditions are no obstacle to universal appeal.

OPPOSITE: Few singers completely dominate a role, but for most of the 1950s and 1960s, della Casa reigned supreme as Richard Strauss's Arabella, a role she recorded twice and as whom she appears in this photograph.

Mario
DEL MONACO

1 9 1 5 – 1 9 8 1

"WHEN IN DOUBT, SHOUT" might have been the maxim of Mario del Monaco, the Italian tenor generally thought to have been the loudest in history. Tradition has it that, in the wake of his victory at a competition held by the Rome Opera School in 1935, the self-taught del Monaco began his singing career with a voice of powerful, but essentially sweet character. However, after marrying his wife, who was said to be hard of hearing, he responded dutifully to her hissed encouragements from the wings that he sing "Louder, Mario! Louder!"

Whatever the reason for his reinvention during the 1940s as the world's leading dramatic *tenore di forza*, del Monaco was unparalleled. Whereas the likes of Franco Corelli and Carlo Bergonzi cultivated and relied upon their technique for vocal security and stamina, del Monaco simply didn't have one, at least not by the standards of his "teachers"—a large collection of his father's 78 rpm LPs.

From his first internationally recognized season in 1945/1946, when he staggered audiences at Verona with his thunderous performances as Radamès (Verdi's *Aida*), del Monaco sang with a lack of restraint that would have ruined any normal voice within 12 months. It was not a beautiful instrument, and yet there have been few singers capable of whipping an audience into the frenzy that greeted del Monaco night after night.

He was not a big man, but when he wanted to, he was capable of drowning out an entire chorus and orchestra. When he was recording, the engineers would have to move him and the microphones around the studio to create an artificial sense of balance. In the theater he was a force of nature, and he stands as one of the few singers to have beaten Maria Callas at her own game. A live recording in 1954 has survived of a performance of Giordano's *Andrea Chénier* at La Scala, in which the audience's hysteria after del Monaco's ear-blistering rendition of "Un dì all'azzurro spazio" so overpowers Callas and the orchestra that the performance has to be halted while the crowd avails itself of its ecstasy.

There was more than a little of the strongman about del Monaco in full flight, and even on record it is easy to imagine a spandex-clad assistant drawing attention to every time-bending high note and aspiritic yelp. Vulgar, tasteless, and insensitive as he was, del Monaco was near perfect in *verismo*, and each of his 427 performances as Verdi's Otello confirmed his status as the indestructible master of that uniquely demanding role.

Ultimately, his influence has been pernicious. Since his heyday in the late 1950s, students have listened to his work with an ear to imitating his blood-and-thunder technique. But del Monaco would not have been able to explain how he did what he did, and many a singer has fallen at the hurdle of imitation. His voice was a phenomenon, and it is best to look back on his work and embrace it for the glorious aberration that it was.

Del Monaco took himself very seriously, but there was always something vaguely unreal and comical about this small-framed man attacking every single note of music "con belto." Here he appears as Verdi's Otello.

Victoria
DE LOS ANGELES

b. 1923

FEW SINGERS HAVE been the focus of such unconditional affection as Spanish soprano Victoria de los Angeles. Her prolonged working life—which spanned her recital debut in 1944 to her performance at the closing ceremony of the Barcelona Olympic Games in 1992—has seen her sing an extraordinary range and variety of music. Although she has specialized in the work of Spanish composers—both on stage and in concert—her effortless technique, acute dramatic sensibilities, and great personal charm have assured her greatness in everything from Mozart, Wagner, and Richard Strauss to Bizet, Massenet, and Puccini. Her recorded legacy remains one of the most popular of the century.

Born in Barcelona, Spain, de los Angeles entered the Conservatorio de Liceo in Barcelona in 1941, where she studied both singing and piano. She completed the six-year course in three years and graduated with full honors when she was only 20. Less than six months after making her concert debut, she appeared for the first time in an opera, as the Countess in *Le nozze di Figaro* (Mozart) at the Gran Teatro Liceo in Barcelona.

This auspicious beginning was crowned in 1947 by her victory at the Geneva International Singing Competition, an achievement that brought her to the attention of the British Broadcasting Corporation (BBC), which invited her to sing the part of Salud in a broadcast production of *La vida breve* (de Falla). Her performance was greatly admired by two other British institutions—the EMI recording company and the English conductor Sir Thomas Beecham.

Having made her Covent Garden debut in 1950, EMI was quick to engage de los Angeles for recordings of *Faust* (Gounod) and *Madama Butterfly* (Puccini), but because Beecham was available for neither production, the longed-for collaboration did not come about until 1956. In that year Beecham conducted de los Angeles as Mimi (opposite Jussi Björling's Rodolfo) in what stands as probably the finest recording of *La bohème* (Puccini) ever made. Beecham, de los Angeles, and EMI were reunited for the second and last time in the studio two years later, when de los Angeles was cast against type as Carmen (Bizet).

Considering the essential delicacy of her soprano, it is a measure of her skills that the performance of this taxing mezzo role works so well. Her reading of Bizet's *femme fatale* benefits from an uncommon class and depth, and it was this intelligent shaping of a character that made each of her performances so special. Thanks partly to her experience as a lieder singer, there was always something intimate in her portrayals, so that even as Nedda (Leoncavallo's *Pagliacci*), her emotions seemed instinctive rather than reactive, as is normally the case. As an artist, de los Angeles was adored because she appeared determined never to impress, and her services to the composer set her apart from many of her more self-conscious, limelight-loving rivals.

The most celebrated Spanish soprano after Montserrat Caballé, de los Angeles was a very different artist, with a delicate, almost childlike demeanor and a light, effortlessly beautiful voice.

Emmy Destinn
als „Carmen"

Emmy
DESTINN

1 8 7 8 – 1 9 3 0

ALTHOUGH SHE SPENT most of her career outside Czechoslovakia, the country of her birth, soprano Emmy Destinn (born Ema Destinnová) was a hero to the Czech nationalist movement. In the 16 years between her debut in 1898 in Berlin, as Santuzza (Mascagni's *Cavalleria rusticana*) and the outbreak of World War I, Destinn was the world's most famous Czech-born woman, achieving cult status throughout Europe and the United States for her exceptional soprano voice and matchless beauty.

In 1914, in a melodramatic act of patriotic heroism, Destinn returned to Prague, where she was almost immediately interned by the occupying Austrian army as a declared Czech nationalist sympathizer. Though a prisoner of her own castle, the principle behind her return, when she could just as easily have remained in the United States, was not lost on the Czech people, and it made her the focus of national respect and admiration.

The decade leading up to repatriation was one of uninterrupted success and triumph. Having won over the Berlin public within a few days of her first appearance there, she became the city's leading prima donna, stunning audiences with her performances as Carmen (Bizet), Mignon (Thomas), Marguerite (Gounod's *Faust*), and, most famously, Salome (Richard Strauss)—her portrayal of which earned her the lifelong devotion of the composer. In 1901 she was chosen by Wagner's widow, Cosima, to sing Senta in a new production of *Der fliegende Holländer*—in which she famously won over the cast, crew, and critics. Three years later she made her now-legendary debut—it caused a sensation—at Covent Garden, as Donna Anna (Mozart's *Don Giovanni*).

In 1908 she traveled to New York for her debut at the Metropolitan. Two years later when Puccini was casting his latest opera, *La fanciulla del West*, he asked Destinn to create the title role, Minnie, in what remains probably the most glittering first night in American operatic history.

Her life after the war was less golden, mainly because it was apparent to everyone except, it seems, Destinn that her powers were in the descendant. There were enough offers, however, to keep the truth at bay, and in 1919 she returned to Covent Garden, singing Verdi's Aida and Amelia in *Un ballo in maschera*. The highlight of her career came shortly after the war's end when she took on the title role of Smetana's flag-waving *Libuše*. Thereafter, her career began to wind down, with sporadic appearances throughout Europe, and even though many anticipated her retirement in her 50th year, no one expected her to die two years after it.

Destinn was a hugely gifted woman. She carried out a voluminous correspondence, wrote plays, and tried her hand at composition. Her more than 200 recordings are highly prized, even though few of them do her uniquely full and flexible soprano justice.

A true star, Destinn was adored on three continents and admired by many of the greatest composers of the day, particularly Puccini. Here she is seen posing as Bizet's Carmen.

Giuseppe
DI STEFANO

b. 1921

THE CAREER OF the Italian tenor Giuseppe di Stefano may well be unique in that he was past his best before he became internationally famous. He made his debut in April 1946, at the Teatro Municipale, Reggio Emilia, as Des Grieux (Massenet's *Manon*). By all accounts, his was the most perfect lyric tenor since the heady days of Fernando de Lucia, and word quickly spread to the manager of La Scala, who booked him without an audition to make his Milanese debut in March 1947. From Milan he came to the attention of the New York Metropolitan, where he first appeared, as the Duke of Mantua (Verdi's *Rigoletto*), in February 1948.

Di Stefano thus progressed from his provincial debut in Parma to the stage of the world's most prestigious opera house in just over two years. For the next five years, his talents were widely proclaimed. The warmth of the voice and his placement of even the most difficult passage work set him apart from the best of his peers, but it was the open-throated naiveté of the voice that made di Stefano such a miraculous, universally loved performer. Half a century on, people still talk of the young di Stefano as the finest lyric tenor of the 20th century. Tragically, however, the greatness of his youth served only to amplify the crisis of his maturity.

In 1952/1953 he began to tire of his repertoire. As a *tenore lirico spinto*, he was restricted to a certain type of role in operas that, while filled with beautiful music, were romantic only in context. The virile, boisterous di Stefano wanted to play the high-dramatic roles that fell, traditionally, to heavier voices, but he had neither the weight, stamina, nor volume to take on the late romantic *verismo* repertory. From having dominated the field as Des Grieux, the Duke of Mantua, Elvino (Bellini's *La sonnambula*), Ernesto (Donizetti's *Don Pasquale*), Arturo (Bellini's *I Puritani*), Wilhelm Meister (Thomas' *Mignon*), Fritz (Mascagni's *L'amico Fritz*), and Nadir (Bizet's *Les pêcheurs de perles*), di Stefano opted to tackle the blood-and-guts repertoire to which he felt temperamentally suited.

Within five years of this disastrous move, his voice was ruined. Between 1953 and 1960, when he made most of his recordings for EMI, di Stefano made more bad repertoire choices than probably any singer before or since. Instead of treasuring his talents, he was tempted into a ludicrous duel with the likes of Mario del Monaco, Carlo Bergonzi, and Franco Corelli—and lost. Spectacularly.

His work from 1960, when he was still not yet 40, was steadily more disappointing. To anyone who had heard him in the 1940s, it was like watching Laurence Olivier forget his lines. Even after his voice was little more than a whisper, he continued to perform, although he was restricted to concert appearances. These continued into the 1990s, but it seems that with the turn of the new millennium, reality has finally taken hold.

"A peasant in a suit" was how one uncharitable critic dismissed di Stefano after one performance during the early 1960s. In his prime, however, di Stefano was gifted with one of the most perfect voices in operatic history.

Plácido
DOMINGO

b. 1941

THE LAST QUARTER of the 20th century produced few operatic icons to compare with those of previous decades, but if one singer has guaranteed his place in the pantheon of operatic greatness, it is the Spanish tenor Plácido Domingo. There have been more refined lyric tenors, more powerful dramatic tenors, tenors with greater ranges, and tenors with more naturally beautiful voices. But there has never been a tenor with the versatility and consistency of Domingo.

Paradoxically, the quality that has made him such a remarkable artist—his versatility—has also been his one consistent weakness. Where ordinary mortals would have been happy to find themselves with a middle-weight dramatic tenor of vitality and beauty, and settled into the Verdian/Puccinian repertoire to which it was quite readily suited, Domingo has had a go at almost every conceivable aspect of the operatic repertoire. He has undertaken a number of roles for which he was suited neither vocally nor temperamentally. Since his career began nearly half a century ago, variety has definitely added spice to his life.

He made his professional debut as a baritone in Mexico City in 1957, but moved up a register four years later, when he made his second debut as Alfredo (Verdi's *La traviata*). For three years from 1962 he was a member of the Israeli National Opera, where he sang some 300 performances. He made his Met debut in 1968 when an indisposed Franco Corelli required him to step in at the last minute as Maurizio (Cilea's *Adriana Lecouvreur*).

ABOVE: Domingo also studied piano and conducting. Here he is conducting a rehearsal of Puccini's La bohème *at the Los Angeles Music Center.*

His international career can be dated from that celebrated event, since which time he has proved to be the world's most consistently reliable tenor. His stamina is a thing of legend. He would happily sing both Turiddu (Mascagni's *Cavalleria rusticana*) and Canio (Leoncavallo's *Pagliacci*) on the same night. Because he would accept almost any challenge—from Mozart, Massenet, Meyerbeer, and Johann Strauss II to Donizetti, Wagner, Puccini, and Richard Strauss—he seemed reluctant to specialize, although the 1970s saw him evolve into a remarkably fine Verdi tenor, notably as Alvaro in *La forza del destino*, Riccardo in *Un ballo in maschera*, Don Carlos, and, most famously, Otello.

Domingo has performed more than 100 different roles, each of which he can sing at a few hours' notice. His great physical strength, fine musicianship, and outstanding dramatic skills led him, during the 1980s, to the operas of Wagner, and aside from his questionable grasp of German, he has proved the outstanding *Heldentenor* of his generation.

OPPOSITE: Here Domingo plays Verdi's Otello at London's Royal Opera House in 1980. The singer has reigned supreme in this role for the last 20 years.

Geraldine
FARRAR

1 8 8 2 – 1 9 6 7

THE AMERICAN SOPRANO Geraldine Farrar was born in Melrose, Massachusetts, the daughter of a baseball player. Her father defied convention by encouraging her musical abilities, and shortly after her 19th birthday, she walked onto the stage of the Berlin Court Opera, where she made her career debut as Marguerite (Gounod's *Faust*). Her performance brought her to the attention of Lilli Lehmann, who took her as a pupil, but after five years in the German capital, Farrar returned to the United States and one of the most glittering careers in American operatic history.

Her arrival in New York was as feverishly anticipated as had been Enrico Caruso's three years earlier. Farrar's debut at the Metropolitan in November 1906, as Juliette (Gounod's *Roméo et Juliette*), did not create the sensation predicted by her admirers, but within five years her fiery spirit, great beauty, realistic approach to stagecraft, and winning voice had made her the Met's leading lyric soprano in a company filled with leading lyric sopranos. In 1910 she was chosen to sing the first performance of Humperdinck's *Königskinder*. Three years later she starred in *Julien*, Charpentier's ill-begotten sequel to *Louise*, and in 1918 she was chosen by Puccini to be the first Suor Angelica.

While these notable events added to her reputation, they were little more than garnish. What made Farrar the most adored American singer of her generation was not her singing but her conspicuous sense of her own equality in a man's world. She made it quite obvious to everyone that she was a match for any man under any circumstances. The public identified with her combative independence, seeing in her public and private convictions something noble to which to aspire. She was the only soprano to give Arturo Toscanini a run for his money (later "enjoying" a famously stormy affair with the conductor). She stood up to Mahler, she slapped Caruso around the Met stage as Carmen (Bizet), and during World War I she made a point of entertaining and protecting German colleagues and friends. The letters of support outweighed the hate-mail five to one.

In her work and choice of roles, she represented nonconformity, independence, and self-knowledge. Women looked on her frank dramatic approach to sexuality with wide-eyed amazement, and everywhere her dramatic skill in roles such as Carmen and Tosca (Puccini) was praised for its theatrical truthfulness.

During the 1910s, when she became the first serious artist to take an interest in film, her fame and popularity were unrivaled. She became the focus for an extraordinary following, mostly of women, known as Gerryflappers, who would mob Farrar at every performance, screaming their devotion from the gods of the Met. She appeared in a dozen movies, and at her retirement in 1922, aged just 40, she was not unreasonably described by the *New York Times* as "America's first superstar: a world-renowned media figure."

Farrar was a woman of exceptional beauty, charisma, and talent. She was justifiably famous as Marguérite (Gounod's Faust*), being one of the few singers able to capture that role's curious mixture of the sacred and the profane.*

Kathleen
FERRIER

1912–1953

FEW OPERA SINGERS achieve international status for their portrayal of just two roles, but like Marian Anderson before her, who only ever sang one, the reputation of English contralto Kathleen Ferrier was founded on quality rather than quantity. Some claim that Ferrier was not, and should not be classed as, an opera singer. Conversely, there are others, such as Benjamin Britten, who thought her one of the most gifted artists of her generation. It is a measure of his faith in her talents that he asked her to make her professional stage debut in the title role of the first performance of his 1946 opera *The Rape of Lucretia*.

The composer's confidence was more than rewarded, as a pirated recording of a performance they gave together in Holland shortly after the Glyndebourne premiere testifies. The following year Glyndebourne engaged her for a new production of *Orfeo* (Gluck), and a glittering operatic career now seemed inevitable. Ferrier, however, preferred working in concert, where she had spent the war years touring the country.

It was through her now-legendary performances of *Das Lied von der Erde* (Mahler) at the 1947 Edinburgh Festival and the 1949 Salzburg Festival that she entered into a prolific collaboration with the conductor Bruno Walter. Having conducted the premiere of *Das Lied von der Erde* in 1911, Walter had high expectations of his soloists, but Ferrier exceeded them wholesale: "No summit of solemnity was inaccessible to her," he recalled, "and it was particularly music of spiritual meaning that seemed her most personal domain."

Another conductor with whom she developed a close working relationship was John Barbirolli, and it was for Ferrier that he mounted a new production of *Orfeo* at Covent Garden, in February 1953. Tragically, she was able to complete only two performances before illness forced her to step down. They were to be her last public appearances, and she died of cancer eight months later, aged 41.

ABOVE: Ferrier making her stage debut in the title role in the first performance of Benjamin Britten's The Rape of Lucretia, *staged at Glyndebourne in 1946.*

Ferrier's voice was one of the 20th century's most unusual. It was almost masculine in its depth and resonance, and there is something peculiarly English in its plummy, expressive fullness. Like Anderson, Ferrier was drawn to her native folk traditions, and it is for her recordings of British songs that she is perhaps best known today.

OPPOSITE: Although she sang only two roles, Ferrier was considered by many, including Benjamin Britten, to be one of the operatic finds of the 20th century. Tragically, her career was cut short before she could reach her full potential.

Dietrich
FISCHER-DIESKAU

b. 1925

IN THE ETERNAL battle between words and music, there have been many casualties, most of them singers. Reconciling the disparate criteria of the poet and the composer is still considered to be the greatest challenge facing an opera singer, particularly those for whom the intimate world of lieder is first love. One of the few postwar singers to have come close to finding the necessary sense of proportion is the German baritone Dietrich Fischer-Dieskau.

During nearly half a century of performances, he covered more ground, with greater success, than almost any other singer of his generation. His skill in the German repertoire—particularly the operas of Wagner and Richard Strauss—was unchallenged. No other male singer paid such attention to the weight, meter, and meaning of operatic verse, yet his successes deluded him into thinking intellect, dramatic intuition, and plastic diction were sufficient to compensate for a lack of voice.

Although Fischer-Dieskau was the leading male vocal actor of his generation, he was by no means the leading baritone, and in spite of a rare sympathy for most of the hundred or so roles to which he applied himself, he was, at heart, doomed always to be a lieder singer in costume.

He sang his first role in the theater in 1947, as Posa in a Berlin State Opera production of Verdi's *Don Carlos*. He remained in Berlin for many years, traveling frequently to Vienna, Salzburg, Bayreuth, and London, where, from 1951, he was arguably the most popular visiting singer. Ten years later he began his long association with contemporary opera, creating the role of Mittenhofer in Henze's *Elegy for Young Lovers*.

During the remaining years of the 1960s, he sang on many of the 20th century's most significant recording projects, including benchmark productions of Busoni's *Doktor Faust*, Berg's *Wozzeck*, and Strauss's *Arabella*. Such was his vocal flexibility, and so complete his mastery of German poetry, that many conductors and producers made the mistake of steering Fischer-Dieskau into areas of repertoire for which he was plainly unsuited.

The voice was not large, and it lacked the necessary weight to navigate successfully many of his favorite non-German roles. As his 1960s recordings of Verdi's *Falstaff* and *Rigoletto* and Puccini's *Tosca* demonstrate, fastidious articulation will get a singer only so far, particularly if it is a "singer's" role. And while in the concert hall Fischer-Dieskau's genius for language made him one of the 20th century's greatest lieder singers, his liking for precious diction was ill suited to the necessarily vulgar and distended arena of romantic Italian opera. He was at his best in those roles, such as Marke (Wagner's *Tristan und Isolde*), in which the relationship between the poetry and the music was at its most even.

Although not everyone appreciated Fischer-Dieskau's performances of Italian repertoire—such as Verdi's Falstaff, as whom he is seen here in a production at the Bavarian State Opera—he was universally respected for his intelligence and integrity—qualities that, ironically, do not always suit the Latin repertoire.

Kirsten
FLAGSTAD

1 8 9 5 – 1 9 6 2

OPERA SINGERS ARE, by nature, rarely as heroic as the characters they play on stage. But with the outbreak of World War II in 1939, all art was politicized, particularly opera, and issues of nationality and allegiance created extraordinary tensions on both sides. One of the most celebrated acts of bravery among singers was the voluntary repatriation of Norwegian soprano Kirsten Flagstad.

When the German army occupied Norway in 1940, Flagstad was in the United States, thrilling audiences with her incomparable performances of the Wagner repertoire. Her choice was simple: remain in the land of the free or return to a German territory solely on account of her husband, the businessman Henry Johansen. In 1941 she chose Johansen, but unbeknown to Flagstad, he had joined the Nazi (Quisling) Party in her absence. When she arrived in Oslo, she was appalled to find herself an honored guest of the Nazi establishment. Showing remarkable bravery, she refused to have anything to do with the occupying forces and successfully persuaded her husband to rescind all formal association with the Quislings.

After the war Johansen was arrested for collaboration and died in 1946 while awaiting trial. Crippled by grief, Flagstad nonetheless returned to singing and, perhaps prematurely, the United States, where she found herself the subject of fierce political argument. Though vilified for having returned to an occupied territory, she stood by her principles. Her strength of character and artistic conviction prevailed, probably because she was still the greatest Wagnerian soprano of the 20th century and even her fiercest critics knew it.

Flagstad made her debut in 1913, in Oslo, where she remained, on and off, for the next 18 years, singing everything from Mozart to Offenbach in her mother tongue. In 1932 she was chosen to sing Wagner's Isolde (*Tristan und Isolde*) in German. Word spread of her success and she was engaged at Bayreuth in 1933 and 1934. There followed invitations from the New York Met, where on February 2, 1935, she made her debut as Sieglinde (Wagner's *Die Walküre*). Four days later she followed this with Isolde, establishing her reputation as the world's leading *Heldensopran*. After the war she sang mostly in concert (including the first performance in 1950 of Richard Strauss's *Four Last Songs*), and whenever she appeared on stage, it was a major international event.

Flagstad's voice was enormous, probably more so than any other soprano of the 20th century, and she used it with uncommon intelligence, achieving a truly Wagnerian synthesis between the words and the music. Her voice always had something of a mezzo character, making it ideal for Brünnhilde (*Der Ring*) and Kundry (*Parsifal*), but in later years it darkened dramatically, and she brought a magical depth to her portrayal of Isolde.

When Flagstad appeared as Dido (Purcell's Dido and Aeneas*) in London in 1951, her contract stated that she was not to boast about the Viking invasion of Britain and that her fee should include a bottle of stout a day.*

Renée
FLEMING

b. 1959

THE EMERGENCE OF American Renée Fleming as the world's most sought-after lyric soprano is a timely reminder that, for all the talk of theatrical veracity and dramatic truth, the love of beauty for beauty's sake is still an influence in contemporary operatic life. Fleming has proved that critics and audiences are no less susceptible to a wonderful voice than they were a century ago. While she is admired for the wit and perception of her characterizations and the intelligence of her acting, Fleming is first and foremost a voice—one of the most impressive since World War II.

Fleming attended the State University of New York (SUNY) at Potsdam, where she studied voice with Patricia Misslin. She graduated in 1981, and soon after began graduate work at the Eastman School of Music in Rochester. Between 1983 and 1987 she attended the Juilliard School's American Opera Center in New York, where she studied with Beverly Johnson. In 1984 she took lessons in Frankfurt with two of her most distinguished predecessors—Dame Elisabeth Schwarzkopf and the late Arleen Augér.

Two years later Fleming made her professional stage debut as Constanze (Mozart's *Die Entführung aus dem Serail*) at the Landestheater in Salzburg. In 1988 she was cast as the Countess in *Le nozze di Figaro* (Mozart), which launched her international career. She made her New York City Opera debut in August 1989, as Mimi (Puccini's *La bohème*) and in December she made her Covent Garden debut as Glauce (Cherubini's *Medée*).

Fleming had been scheduled to make her New York Metropolitan Opera debut in 1992, but it was brought forward unexpectedly when, in 1991, she was asked to replace an indisposed Felicity Lott as the Countess in *Le nozze di Figaro*—by now her signature role and as whom she made her debuts in San Francisco, Vienna, Geneva, and Glyndebourne. In 1995 she sang her first Marschallin (Richard Strauss's *Der Rosenkavalier*) at the Houston Grand Opera. She takes an interest in contemporary music and has performed in the world premieres of three operas. In 1991 she created the role of the Countess in *The Ghosts of Versailles* (Corigliano) at the Met, in 1994 she appeared as Madam de Tourvel in the world premiere of *The Dangerous Liaisons* (Susa) in San Francisco, and in September 1998 she premiered the role of Blanche DuBois in *A Streetcar Named Desire* (André Previn) at the San Francisco Opera.

Fleming's warm, gloriously rich soprano is, by nature, limited to a small range of music, but she has excelled in many languages: the title role in *Rusalka* (Dvořák), Tatyana (Tchaikovsky's *Eugene Onegin*), Ellen Orford (Britten's *Peter Grimes*), Desdemona (Verdi's *Otello*), and Marguerite (Gounod's *Faust*). She has an unrivaled adaptability to music that has normally not benefited from an instrument as opulent as Fleming's. Having achieved so much, it will be fascinating to see how her career develops from here.

*Fleming as Mozart's Countess (*Le nozze di Figaro*)—the role that unexpectedly launched her international career as the world's leading lyric soprano.*

Mirella
FRENI

b. 1935

THE ITALIAN LOVE affair with the voice has found no more seductive focus for its devotion than soprano Mirella Freni. She is, in most respects, the antithesis of Maria Callas, whose voice bordered on the ugly but who could carry a role thanks to a mixture of melodramatic conviction and theatrical technique. Freni is almost entirely voice, and her stellar career can be attributed to the unpretentious, priceless beauty of her lyric soprano.

When the conductor Herbert von Karajan heard her sing for the first time, he remembered being awestruck by the smoothness and clarity of the instrument. He knew better than anyone that her qualities were lyric rather than dramatic, and during the 1960s, when they were regular partners, he would extend her unique latitude, indulging the voice for want, perhaps, of any real sense of character.

Freni made her unofficial debut in 1945, aged 10, when she sang an aria from *La traviata* (Verdi) in a radio competition for children. The performance was heard by Beniamino Gigli, who recommended that she stop singing or run the risk of ruining her voice before it had a chance to mature. She immediately retired, waiting until she was 17 before beginning her vocal studies afresh.

Three years later she made her debut, as Micaëla (Bizet's *Carmen*), in her native city, Modena. In 1957 she became the first Italian singer in nearly a decade to win the Viotti International competition, which led to a season with the Netherlands Opera and her Glyndebourne debut as Zerlina (Mozart's *Don Giovanni*). In 1961 she was cast as Nannetta by Zeffirelli for his Covent Garden production of *Falstaff* (Verdi).

It was Karajan, though, who elevated her status when, in 1963, he chose her to sing Mimi (Puccini's *La bohème*) in Vienna. From then on, Freni was the leading Italian lyric soprano, scoring triumphs throughout Europe and the United States and on numerous recordings, including celebrated interpretations, alongside Karajan and Pavarotti, of Puccini's *La bohème* (1972) and *Madama Butterfly* (1974).

Even though Freni is no great actress, relying as she does on vocal tone for effect, her career represents the apogee of discipline. As a born lyric soprano, she has paced herself with extraordinary discretion, so that even when offers came flooding in for her to learn heavier roles (including one rejected offer from Karajan for her to sing Puccini's Turandot), she adhered strictly to the repertoire that she knew to be suited to her voice. Only when she knew her voice could cope did she turn to the Verdian *spinto* roles, in which she excelled, of Desdemona (*Otello*), Elisabeth de Valois (*Don Carlos*), and Amelia (*Simon Boccanegra*). In recent years she has turned to Tchaikovsky's heroines Tatyana (*Eugene Onegin*) and Lisa (*Queen of Spades*) with success, and she continues to learn new roles (such as Giordano's Fedora and Madame Sans-Gêne) without ever placing her voice at risk.

*During the 1970s, when she was at her prime, Freni's appearances as Puccini's Mimi (*La bohème*) and Madama Butterfly (as whom she is seen here) secured her a reputation as one of the finest lyric sopranos of the century.*

Mary
GARDEN
1874–1967

THERE HAVE BEEN few operatic lives more curious than that of Scottish-born soprano Mary Garden. Her family emigrated to the United States when she was a child, and she studied singing in Chicago and Paris before becoming the darling of the Parisian operatic world and the apple of Debussy's eye.

In 1900 she was engaged by Albert Carré of the Opéra Comique in Paris, where she took over the title role of Charpentier's hit *Louise* after Marthe Rioton fell ill. After seeing Garden as Louise, Debussy was smitten and he insisted that she create Mélisande in the first performance of his opera *Pelléas et Mélisande* in 1902. Between them, Carré, Debussy, and Garden helped turn the potentially disastrous work into the season's jewel, and the composer remained eternally devoted to his "Scottish soprano."

Garden's services to Charpentier and Debussy were not unique. Many other French composers benefited from her open mind and intuitive artistry. She sang numerous of Massenet's operas, including a particularly celebrated portrayal of Manon, the intensity of which prompted the composer to write *Chérubin* especially for her. Garden dutifully gave the first performance in Monte Carlo in 1905. The following year she created the role of Aphrodite in D'Erlanger's *Camille*, and in 1907 she made her American debut as Massenet's Thaïs, creating a sensation that brought her enormous celebrity and wealth.

Her preference for the good things in life was legendary, and when in 1921 she was chosen to become director of the Chicago Opera, Garden oversaw one of the most profligate seasons in operatic history. Having worked for Oscar Hammerstein in Manhattan, Garden saw it as her duty to apply his famously extravagant standards in Chicago. She shipped in star performers for single performances, engaged the most expensive designers, and staged new works with no discernible popular appeal—most famously the first production of Prokofiev's *The Love for Three Oranges*.

Garden's first and only season as manager ended, according to the *Chicago Tribune*, in "magnificent smashing ruin," and Garden was politely asked to concentrate, in future, on singing. This she did, to varying degrees of success, into the 1930s, when she crowned her career with two final American premieres—Honegger's *Judith* and Alfano's *Risurezzione*. Her voice can be heard on numerous recordings—she made her first in 1903, of Debussy's songs, with the composer at the piano—but they do her no great justice.

She was a lyric rather than a dramatic soprano, although she did sing the first American Salome (Richard Strauss) in 1909. According to most of those who saw her on stage, she was very much a singing actress, for whom the composer's music was never more than a means to enhancing the poet's words, which explains Debussy's admiration and her lasting success when, according to most sources, her voice was past its best as early as 1907.

During her lifetime Garden was one of the most devoted and successful servants of contemporary music. This publicity photograph taken in the early 1900s shows Garden in an unnamed role.

Nicolai
GEDDA

b. 1925

THE SWEDISH TENOR Nicolai Gedda seems never to have known what sort of tenor he was. He has been a *Spieltenor*, a *lyrischer Tenor*, a French *ténor*, a *ténor trial*, a *ténor-bouffe*, a *tenore di grazia*, a *tenore spinto*, and a *tenor-buffo*. In fact, the only categories in which Gedda has not specialized are those of which he is physically incapable—the Italian *tenore di forza* and the German *Heldentenor*. At one time or another, Gedda has performed in every other tenor register and, as such, he is probably the only singer of the 20th century to have specialized in everything.

It would take a great deal more space than is available here to catalog his more than 100 roles, which span three centuries of musical history, half a dozen languages—each of which he speaks fluently—and every conceivable style from the light comedy of Rossini and Adam to the heavy intricacies of Pfitzner and Orff.

Although he is a naturally light tenor, albeit with a huge range up to a high D, Gedda's repertoire has embraced an eye-popping variety. On record alone, mostly in the 1950s and 1960s, he has performed the lead tenor roles in Puccini's *La bohème* and *Madama Butterfly*, Massenet's *Manon* and *Werther*, Tchaikovsky's *Eugene Onegin*, Gluck's *Orfeo*, a whole stableful of Mozart, the standard Verdi, Bellini's *I Puritani*, Bizet's *Carmen* and *Les pêcheurs de perles*, Johann Strauss's *Die Fledermaus*, Richard Strauss's *Capriccio*, Mussorgsky's *Boris Godounov*, Prokofiev's *War and Peace*, Rossini's *Il barbiere di Siviglia*, Bernstein's *Candide*, and everything by Berlioz. His open mind has accommodated a number of contemporary operas, including the world premieres of Orff's *Trionfo di Afrodite*, Barber's *Vanessa*, and Menotti's *The Last Savage*.

It might be expected that a "jack" of so many trades would be doomed to remain a master of none. But Gedda has constantly defied expectation, and with the exception of his forays into the romantic Italian repertoire—specifically the operas of Verdi and Puccini, his performances of which have never satisfied—Gedda has proved to be expert in almost everything to which he has applied himself. As a Mozart stylist he is unrivaled, and no other tenor of his generation has so completely attuned himself to the character of Berlioz's operas, his 1970s recordings of which under the baton of conductor Colin Davis remain one of the glories of the 20th century.

At his best, Gedda could soar the heights of bel canto (as in his celebrated performances of Adam's pyrotechnical *Le postillon de Longjumeau*), and in the right music, such as Pfitzner's *Palestrina*, he was an artist of rare profundity. Gedda's versatility has done neither his voice nor his career any harm, and since sailing past his 70th birthday—into his fifth decade as a professional singer—he has shown no sign of retiring.

Like Dietrich Fischer-Dieskau, Gedda was not always successful in romantic Italian opera, but he was gifted with a superb voice and perceptive dramatic instincts—mandatory for the role of the Duke of Mantua in Verdi's Rigoletto, *as whom he is seen here in a production in Munich in 1966.*

Beniamino
GIGLI
1890–1957

"APART FROM MY VOICE, I am a very ordinary person." Italian tenor Beniamino Gigli's claim to normalcy was fair, but only up to a point. He was first and foremost a singer, albeit with no discernible dramatic instincts or acting skills. He was a modest man who cultivated immodest tastes and he lived a life defined by purely musical achievements.

Only twice was he called upon to be extraordinary. The first occasion was in 1932 when, having sung at the Metropolitan Opera in New York for 12 consecutive seasons, he was asked to accept a pay cut, brought on by the Depression. He refused—one of only two singers to do so, the other being Giacomo Lauri-Volpi—and left the United States for Italy, where he faced the second great test of his character. With the dictator Mussolini and the Fascists in office, Gigli opted to ally himself, through performance and patronage, to the Fascisti. Thereafter, he became a favorite of the Italian dictator's, and performed on numerous occasions for Hitler, Goebbels, and the Nazi hierarchy.

It is a measure of his standing with the public that he was so readily forgiven his conduct after World War II, although the Italian public took longer than most to forget. In March 1945 he returned to Rome Opera as Cavaradossi (Puccini's *Tosca*), and to Covent Garden in February 1946 as Rodolfo (Puccini's *La bohème*).

The critics were routinely offended by Gigli's sentimental mannerisms, but as the singer was the first to admit, he was not performing for his critics. He regarded himself as "the people's singer," and his desire for popular acclaim goes some way toward explaining his appearance in no less than 24 movies. If Gigli never attempted to disguise the fact that he knew little English and had almost no talent for acting, then it is equally fair to say that audiences weren't interested in his speaking voice.

His hundreds of recordings over four decades continue to sell in their thousands, including eight complete performances of his best-known roles—Canio (Leoncavallo's *Pagliacci*), Rodolfo (*La bohème*), Cavaradossi (*Tosca*), Pinkerton (Puccini's *Madama Butterfly*), Turiddu (Mascagni's *Cavalleria rusticana*), Riccardo (Verdi's *Un ballo in maschera*), Radamès (Verdi's *Aida*), and Andrea Chénier (Giordano).

Gigli was clearly one of the greatest tenors of the 20th century, and many consider him second only to Enrico Caruso. Yet, as Gigli candidly admitted in his memoirs, he may well have been the elder tenor's equal as a singer, but he had none of those "gifts of personality that enabled Caruso to create life and warmth around him wherever he went."

BELOW: Gigli practicing at the Savoy in 1954 during his farewell tour of the United Kingdom.

OPPOSITE: Gigli was capable of singing almost anything, and practically did, performing a huge number of roles in a career that spanned five decades.

Tito
GOBBI

1913–1984

If Maria Callas was the greatest singing actress of her day, then the greatest singing actor was Italian baritone Tito Gobbi. He was a sensation almost from the outset when, at the tender age of 22, he won an international singing competition in Vienna. Gobbi enjoyed almost no apprenticeship and was singing the major baritone roles by Verdi, Donizetti, and Bellini within months of making his Rome Opera debut in June 1937. In Rome he was adopted by the legendary conductor Tullio Serafin, who in 1942 took the extraordinary step of giving Gobbi the title role in the Italian premiere of Berg's *Wozzeck*.

Gobbi's acute dramatic instincts and genius for declamation—cultivated by way of compensation for what was, by contemporary standards, a small voice—led to a reputation for skill with contemporary music. He was "honored" with the creation of numerous new works, including roles in operas by Rocca, Malipiero, Persico, Lualdi, Napoli, and Ghedini. By 1951, when he made his Covent Garden debut as Belcore in Donizetti's *L'elisir d'amore*, Gobbi was the favored baritone not only of Serafin but also of Callas and EMI. Between them, Gobbi, Callas, Serafin, and EMI collaborated on some of the most important recordings of the 20th century, most famously of all *Tosca* (Puccini, 1953), but also *Rigoletto* (Verdi, 1955), and *Il barbiere di Siviglia* (Rossini, 1957).

While Gobbi preferred the opera house to the studio, recording nonetheless highlighted his remarkable skills as a vocal actor, just as the microphone compensated for his vocal limitations. Of course, it could be argued that his ambivalent pitching, uneven vibrato, and rugged phrasing were what made him such a great operatic singer, and it would be difficult to imagine any baritone approaching the role of Baron Scarpia (*Tosca*), for example, without having first absorbed Gobbi's portrayal.

The hallmark of great singers is that they never leave an audience feeling indifferent, and while many disapproved of Gobbi's eye-rolling ham theatrics and parlando technique—one critic famously commented that Gobbi was "Titta Ruffo without a voice"—an audience never left a performance by Gobbi uncertain of the role's dimensions.

Although he continued into the late 1960s, on occasion directing his own productions, Gobbi was a child of the 1930s, when the likes of Giovanni Martinelli and Giuseppe de Luca were at the peak of their fame. On every level Gobbi was their superior as an actor, but he never deviated from their stylized, antinaturalist conception of the theater as an artificial environment. For as long as an audience accepted this, and left its credulity at the cloakroom, Gobbi was one of the most captivating performers of the 20th century. Gobbi treated opera as the distorted, unrealistic art form that it is, and his legacy continues to haunt those among his heirs who, for whatever reason, see in opera the hope of reason and reality.

No picture better captures Gobbi's gloriously exaggerated and distended approach to opera than this splendid shot of him in character as Verdi's Falstaff in Franco Zeffirelli's production for Covent Garden in 1961.

Marilyn
HORNE

b. 1934

AMONG THE MANY operatic virtuosos who have come to prominence since World War II, arguably the most virtuosic of them all is the American mezzo-soprano Marilyn Horne. Her peerless technique and prodigious range enabled her to sing an unparalleled spectrum of music—from Bach, Mozart, and Rossini to Wagner, Mahler, and Berg—with consummate ease and security.

This versatility has seen her undertake extraordinary feats of vocal discipline. Her reputation, however, is founded on her being the only American mezzo-soprano to have mastered, by Italian standards, the florid bel canto method required for the singing of Rossini, Bellini, and Donizetti. As such, she is one of the very few opera stars to have turned versatility to her advantage.

Horne first came to public attention as one of Lotte Lehmann's pupils in Santa Barbara, but it was for her performance of the title role—mimed by Dorothy Dandridge—in the 1954 film of Oscar Hammerstein's *Carmen Jones* that Horne achieved popular recognition. The previous summer she had made her theatrical debut in Los Angeles, later coming to the attention of Igor Stravinsky, who invited her to the 1956 Venice Festival. From Venice Horne moved to the Gelsenkirchen company in Germany, singing both mezzo and soprano roles, including Mimi (Puccini's *La bohème*), Giulietta (Offenbach's *Les contes d'Hoffmann*), and Amelia (Verdi's *Simon Boccanegra*). In 1960 she achieved one of the greatest successes of her career when, at the inauguration of Gelsenkirchen's new opera house, she sang the role of Marie (Berg's *Wozzeck*).

This remarkable portrayal led her back to the United States, and her debut in San Francisco, again as Marie. But in 1961 she performed for the first time with Australian soprano Joan Sutherland, as Agnese to Sutherland's Beatrice (Bellini's *Beatrice di Tenda*), and overnight she found herself transformed from an operatic all-rounder, with a leaning toward 20th-century music, into a 19th-century bel canto specialist. Again singing opposite Sutherland, Horne was outstanding as Arsace (Rossini's *Semiramide*) and Adalgisa (Bellini's *Norma*), to say nothing of her extraordinary performances in Donizetti's *Lucrezia Borgia* and *Anna Bolena*, and in Rossini's *L'italiana in Algeri* and *Il barbiere di Siviglia*.

For her portrayal of Rosina (*Il barbiere di Siviglia*), Horne would span three registers, from contralto to soprano, accommodating extremes of pitch while remaining in control of an arsenal of vocal effects, including trills, chromatic runs, breathless legatos, and improvised cadenzas. If she sometimes overdid the pyrotechnics, then she was, at least, their master, and the only casualty of her bag of tricks was the composer, since many of her embellishments added little to the drama and frequently distracted from it. If a singer can ever have been said to have been too good, then Marilyn Horne is a leading candidate.

Widely admired as one of the most complete vocal technicians of the 20th century, Horne developed an almost mechanical virtuosity that enabled her to sing almost anything.

Hans
HOTTER

b. 1909

BEFORE HIS 21ST BIRTHDAY, the German bass-baritone Hans Hotter had studied music and philosophy, worked as a professional choral singer, a church organist, a choirmaster, and, in 1930, made his professional stage debut as an opera singer in Troppau. The ensuing 70 years have seen little decline in his apparently limitless reserves of energy and invention. Although he retired from the stage in 1972, he has continued to work as a producer, narrator, and, on increasingly rare occasions, a singer. Even Hotter concedes that his ninth decade has seen a dilution of his great physical strength and vocal substance.

Hotter was a legend before he achieved international celebrity during the 1950s thanks to his landmark performances of Wagner in Bayreuth, Vienna, London, Munich, and New York. In 1937 the conductor Clemens Krauss offered Hotter a guest contract to sing with his company in Munich. With the Nazis running the country, and with Munich Opera known to be one of the government's most visible pawns, Hotter knew what he was letting himself in for. But like many of his colleagues, he was politically naive and found himself distracted from the truth of his situation by one of Krauss's friends, the composer Richard Strauss.

In 1938 Strauss urged Krauss to cast Hotter as the Kommandant in the first performance of his "peace opera," *Friedenstag*. It was an honor of immeasurable significance for the singer, who went from being one of the composer's admirers to arguably his most committed disciple. Four years later, by which stage he had added most of Strauss's major baritone roles to his repertoire, Hotter was asked to create the role of Olivier in the premiere of *Capriccio*. In 1944 he helped bring down the curtain on Strauss's operatic career when he sang Jupiter in the first performance of *Die Liebe der Danae*. These honors gave Hotter a rare, almost unique place in Strauss's affections, and it was somehow fitting that he should eventually have married into the composer's family.

After World War II Hotter became a regular feature of Wieland Wagner's New Bayreuth, and during the 1950s and 1960s, he straddled the globe as the finest Wagner bass-baritone in living memory. His magnificent voice—which, as Wagner had stipulated, was a true bass-baritone with both the necessary weight and depth as well as the range and flexibility—and superior intelligence made him unforgettable as Hans Sachs (Wagner's *Die Meistersinger*) and irreplaceable as Wotan (Wagner's *Der Ring*).

No other singer so captured the grandeur of Wagner's creations, and while he was unrivaled as Borromeo (Pfitzner's *Palestrina*), Mandryka (Strauss's *Arabella*), and Jokanaan (Strauss's *Salome*), it was for his Wagner that Hotter will be remembered. The declamatory power, vocal coloring, breathless phrasing, and eloquent characterizations created a standard to which every operatic actor has since aspired—an aspiration as yet unsatisfied.

Uniquely diverse, Hotter brought refinement and sophistication to areas of the repertoire that were normally submerged beneath cliché and platitude. Here he plays Dr. Bartolo in Rossini's Il barbiere di Siviglia.

Maria
JERITZA

1 8 8 7 – 1 9 8 2

THOUGH BORN IN MORAVIA, soprano Maria Jeritza will forever be associated with Vienna, where, for more than 20 years, she was the city's leading prima donna and the finest singing actress of her generation. As celebrated for her extraordinary talents as for her exalted lifestyle, Jeritza enjoyed phenomenal prominence in a city that at the time was almost mythically saturated with genius.

She was feted by royalty, loved by the public, and venerated by her peers. Significantly, she was idolized by many of Europe's most prominent composers, including Puccini, Mascagni, Janáček, Korngold, and Richard Strauss. In this context she was arguably the last great soprano to have established her reputation, and achieved international popularity, through the performance of contemporary music.

Fittingly, she made her debut at the Vienna Staatsoper in 1912 in a performance of Oberleithner's *Aphrodite*. The role was tailor-made for Jeritza, since it was generally agreed that she was one of the most beautiful women ever to have graced the stage of an opera house. Only a few months later, she was invited by Strauss to create the title role in *Ariadne auf Naxos* in Stuttgart. She returned to the role when Strauss's revision of the opera was premiered in Vienna four years later.

Having scored a huge success for Strauss, she did much the same on a regular basis for Puccini; as his Tosca and Minnie (*Tosca* and *La fanciulla del West*) she was thought by the composer to be among the greatest he had ever seen. In the former role she was uniquely forceful, if not downright flamboyant. Aside from the remarkable physicality and sexual menace of her portrayal, she would sing "Vissi d'arte" lying on the floor, and her murder of Scarpia was said to have caused gasps from audiences who thought they knew exactly what to expect.

In 1919 Strauss asked her to create the role of the Empress in *Die Frau ohne Schatten*, and the following year she helped score an international success for the 23-year-old Korngold when she created the role of Marie/Marietta in the premiere of *Die tote Stadt*. Less than a year later, Jeritza was summoned to New York, where she gave the American premiere of Korngold's masterpiece. For the next 12 seasons she reigned supreme as the Metropolitan Opera's most beautiful and glamorous star.

Jeritza remained committed to new music, performing in the first American production of Janáček's *Jenůfa* in 1924, singing the title role in the first American *Turandot* (Puccini) in 1926, and in 1928 the first American Helen in the New York premiere of *Die ägyptische Helena* (Strauss). A true singing actress, Jeritza lived to 94, long enough for her to see the rise and fall of Maria Callas, the only soprano ever thought to have matched Jeritza's skills on the stage, and her magnetism off it.

Jeritza was one of the true goddesses of the operatic stage, as adored for her beauty as for her singing, both of which gave her the pick of contemporary opera, famously the works of Richard Strauss, Puccini, and Korngold.

Siegfried
JERUSALEM

b. 1940

LEGEND HAS IT that after the retirement of Wolfgang Windgassen in the early 1970s, Wolfgang Wagner, director of the Bayreuth Festival, placed a sign on the door of the theater announcing: "Closed until a tenor is found." Fortunately for the world's major Wagner-producing cities, a young German bassoonist named Siegfried Jerusalem was persuaded to train his voice in tandem with his duties as an orchestral musician. When the conductor Sergiu Celibidache counseled Jerusalem, "Sit no more in the orchestra. You are a singer," Jerusalem abandoned the pit for the stage.

Having had no formal voice training, and having already passed his 30th birthday, Jerusalem promised little. But working his way through the lyric repertoire—chiefly in the operas of Mozart, Beethoven, Weber, and Verdi, and the operettas of Johann Strauss and Lehár—he cultivated a technique of impregnable security, to which he brought an acute musical intelligence, a sensitive dramatic facility, and a handsome stage presence.

After periods in Hamburg and Darmstadt, Jerusalem was invited by Wolfgang Wagner to Bayreuth, where he made his solo debut as Wagner's Lohengrin in 1975. Although the critics were initially divided as to his merits, Jerusalem was quite obviously the natural heir to Windgassen's throne, and over the next 20 years, he came to dominate the German repertoire, particularly as Lohengrin and his own namesake, Siegfried (*Der Ring*).

While the shortage of Wagner tenors is as much a problem today as it was in the 1970s, Jerusalem has, like the boy with his finger in the dike, almost single-handedly sustained the traditions of the German Wagner tenor. As evidence for this can be quoted his appearance as Siegfried on four of the last five complete recordings of the *Ring* cycle.

His voice is not big—at least not when compared to those of James King or Jon Vickers—but big is not necessarily better, and Jerusalem has proved that stamina, beauty of tone, musicianship, and articulate diction will always serve Wagner's intentions better than volume per se. Furthermore, the open-throated elegance, color, placement, and range (up to a high C) of Jerusalem's voice allow him a flexibility that no other German tenor since World War II has brought to the Wagner repertoire.

As it is, his voice has darkened considerably over the years, and his work at Bayreuth with conductor Daniel Barenboim, which culminated in 1993 in the finest recording of *Götterdämmerung* ever made, has reached a level of perfection unheard since the prewar days of Franz Völker and Max Lorenz. When, during the 1980s, Jerusalem progressed to the heavier roles of Siegmund (*Die Walküre*), Tristan (*Tristan und Isolde*), and Parsifal, many questioned his suitability to the repertoire. But he has consistently proved himself the finest *Heldentenor* of his generation, particularly at Bayreuth where, having retired from the festival in 1999, he leaves the theater once again "closed until a tenor is found."

The last of the great German Heldentenors, Jerusalem has now bid farewell to Bayreuth, leaving the theater once more "closed until a tenor is found."

Gwyneth
JONES
b. 1937

AT HER BEST, between 1964 and 1972, Welsh soprano Gwyneth Jones possessed one of the most beautiful soprano voices of the postwar era. But since she was naturally a mezzo-soprano, in which register she began her career in 1962, it was hardly a surprise that the pressures of singing outside her natural range should have finished her voice, if not her career, some 20 years sooner than might normally have been expected.

The villain of the tale was Nello Santi, the music director of Zurich Opera, where Jones was engaged from 1962. He persuaded her that she was a soprano, and a dramatic soprano at that, and with his "guidance," she shifted up a gear for her soprano debut, as Amelia (Verdi's *Un ballo in maschera*). During the next few years she concentrated on the Italian repertoire, chiefly the operas of Verdi. It was as Leonora in Verdi's *Il trovatore* that Jones leaped to British celebrity in 1964, when she was called upon to replace an indisposed Leontyne Price at Covent Garden. In quick succession, she added Verdi's Desdemona (*Otello*), Elisabeth de Valois (*Don Carlos*), Aida, and Lady Macbeth (*Macbeth*), as well as Puccini's Tosca and Madama Butterfly and Mascagni's Santuzza (*Cavalleria rusticana*) to her successes. While most of these roles forced her outside her natural range, her performances were exceptional for their power, intelligence, and beauty.

A few weeks after her appearance at Covent Garden, Jones was asked to substitute for another indisposed singer, as Leonore in *Fidelio* (Beethoven), and from then on it was for her performances of the German repertoire that Jones was internationally recognized. Conductor Karl Böhm hailed her as one of the finest Salomes (Strauss) of his career. She was Leonard Bernstein's favorite Octavian (Strauss's *Der Rosenkavalier*), and conductor Carlos Kleiber insisted that she sing the Marschallin (*Der Rosenkavalier*) for him in Vienna. Eventually, she progressed to Wagner, working her way through Gutrune (*Götterdämmerung*) and Sieglinde (*Die Walküre*), before finally navigating Brünnhilde (*Der Ring*).

In 1968 Jones first sang at Bayreuth where, four years later, she established a precedent for sopranos to double as Elisabeth and Venus (Wagner's *Tannhäuser*). In 1976, when her voice had lost much of its beauty, Wolfgang Wagner chose her to sing Brünnhilde as part of the centenary *Ring*. Admiring though many were of the depth of her interpretation, few could deny that the pressures of singing outside her means had left Jones with a voice that was not even a shadow of its former glory. Within little more than a decade, potentially the most gifted mezzo of her generation had risen to glory at Bayreuth as a soprano, only to spend the rest of her career fighting off her critics.

Jones continues to draw crowds for her performances as Puccini's Turandot and Minnie (*La fanciulla del West*). Whether her resilience is courageous or delusional, the trajectory of her career provides confirmation that the worst of the vices is advice.

Jones may not have been meant to sing the Heldensopran *repertoire, but early in her career, famously as Sieglinde (Wagner's* Die Walküre*) at Bayreuth, as pictured here, she was revered for the power and richness of her performances.*

Alfredo
KRAUS

1 9 2 7 – 1 9 9 9

IF THE DELPHIC temple's cardinal invocation "Know Thyself" is the ultimate requisite for a successful and fulfilled life, then the Spanish tenor Alfredo Kraus was one of the most successful and fulfilled singers of the 20th century. Unlike his better-known "Three Tenors" colleagues, Kraus demonstrated an exemplary awareness of his natural limitations as a singer and worked within them for nearly 50 years.

Krauss's discipline as an artist was without equal, and so secure was he within himself that he never attempted to alter or remold his art in the light of fashion, financial temptation, personal insecurity, or simple boredom. From the outset Kraus was under no illusions as to the sort of tenor he was. It was not a big voice and, unusually, it never darkened during its working life, remaining as smooth and elegant at the end as at the beginning, when he made his formal debut, in 1956, as the Duke of Mantua (Verdi's *Rigoletto*) in Cairo.

He developed his repertoire with an ear to its suitability, first and foremost, to his voice. As much as he would have loved to have played Manrico (Verdi's *Il trovatore*), Calaf (Puccini's *Turandot*), and Andrea Chénier (Giordano), he knew that he was simply not the right vehicle for these heavier roles, and abstained. Instead, he worked on mastering a small, ideally suited repertoire, perhaps 20 roles in total, to which he could bring a perfect technique and uncommon insight. Although he was perfectly comfortable in the light romantic Italian repertoire, and outstanding as, among others, Arturo (Bellini's *I Puritani*), Nemorino (Donizetti's *L'elisir d'amore*), and Alfredo (Verdi's *La traviata*), it was as a French *ténor* that he excelled. No other postwar singer brought such charm, elegance, and style to the operas of Gounod, Massenet, Bizet, and Offenbach. As Faust (Gounod), Roméo (Gounod's *Roméo et Juliette*), Des Grieux (Massenet's *Manon*), *Werther* (Massenet), Nadir (Bizet's *Les pêcheurs de perles*), and Hoffmann (Offenbach's *Les contes d'Hoffmann*), he tapped a vein of melancholy lyricism that connected him to the long and, until his emergence, broken line of prewar French stylists.

Kraus's performances were not, however, to everyone's tastes, and he was excluded from the media circus that inflated the standing of the tenor during the 1980s and 1990s. He was not popular with his tenor rivals, and his lack of popular acclaim in no way affected his prestige as a star among committed opera-lovers.

Kraus was one of 20th-century opera's true aristocrats. A singer's singer, eternally youthful, and blessed with brains as well as voice, he was an artist for the connoisseur, providing object lessons in sensitivity, dignity, economy, and integrity. Above all, he was a singer whose understanding of his craft enabled him to create an art worthy of respect, and it would not be going too far to suggest that his death, in his 72nd year, robbed the opera world of one of its youngest and most promising stars.

Kraus brought exceptional refinement and artistry to the lyric tenor repertoire, particularly the lighter end of the bel canto repertoire. Here he is seen in costume as the Duke of Mantua (Verdi's Rigoletto*) at the New York Met in 1974.*

Mario
LANZA

1921–1959

ITALIAN-AMERICAN TENOR Mario Lanza was the first singer, popular or otherwise, to earn gold records, with million sellers in both classical and popular categories. In addition his MGM hit, *The Great Caruso*, was the highest grossing film of 1951. To cap it all, the conductor Arturo Toscanini announced to the world that Lanza's was the "voice of the century." Yet the world of opera has dismissed the talent, life, and work of Lanza, and such snobbery is one of its most lasting shames.

Lanza's name is routinely omitted from opera dictionaries, histories, and compendiums. There are common excuses for overlooking Lanza's unparalleled contribution to opera in the 20th century. Some claim that because he never sang a complete role in an opera house, he cannot therefore be considered an opera singer, which is a little like claiming that a painter is only ever an artist when his or her work has been shown. Others maintain that his voice was coarse and that he used it to play to the gallery, as if those paragons of tenor virtue, Giacomo Lauri-Volpi and Mario del Monaco, did anything else. The bleakest reason for denying his existence is the one to which most of his critics will no longer admit: that Lanza was a populist, and that through his film work, it is claimed, he cheapened the hallowed halls of operatic tradition. The truth, of course, is that Lanza did most to bring opera to more people than any other singer, before or since.

His life story is quite as remarkable as that of Enrico Caruso, whom Lanza portrayed in *The Great Caruso*. He was born Alfred Arnold Cocozza in South Philadelphia. In 1940 he sang for the conductor Sergey Koussevitsky, who immediately arranged for the 19-year-old to sing at Tanglewood. Having spent World War II as "the Caruso of the Air Force," touring U.S. bases, he embarked on a concert career as Mario Lanza. RCA Victor signed him to record soon after, but the biggest break of his career came when he was engaged to substitute for Ferruccio Tagliavini at a Hollywood Bowl Concert on August 28, 1947. An MGM film contract, and meteoric rise to stardom, followed soon after.

Lanza was given his own national radio show, appeared on countless magazine covers, and became the public incarnation of the operatic tenor. In the 1950s and for many years after, when most Americans thought of opera, they thought of Lanza, which, considering the ringing power and erotic beauty of the voice, was no bad thing. But Lanza lived life to extremes, and his fame, and the expectation of audiences, led him into manic depression, prescription drugs, alcoholism, overeating, sexual excesses, and professional rancor. He also ran into the Mob, and one such dispute, with Charles "Lucky" Luciano, is said to have led to Lanza's death at the age of 38. The official line is that he died from a heart attack, which, considering his lifestyle, was probably the more likely cause of death. Either way, it was a tragedy for the operatic world, even if it has still yet to realize it.

Loved and admired in equal measure, Lanza challenged convention and prejudice with a boldness and natural talent unprecedented in American operatic history. He is seen here as Marc Revere in the 1958 film The Seven Hills of Rome.

Giacomo
LAURI-VOLPI

1892–1979

IT IS NO COINCIDENCE that a good number of the 20th century's most revered Italian tenors were also among its most vulgar, and the patron saint of questionable judgment was Italian tenor Giacomo Lauri-Volpi. While purists will always recoil from the sort of "cheap" tricks and devices mastered by "gallery" tenors, there is no denying the thrill of a singer with bad taste in good form.

Lauri-Volpi made his debut, in 1919, in Viterbo under the pseudonym Giacomo Rubini—the name of Bellini's favorite tenor—which endeared him to few. But the many were wholly seduced by the young man's obvious talents, and even if he seemed terribly pleased with himself, there was no denying the value of a high tenor with audience appeal.

His progress was extraordinarily swift. Having reverted to his birth name, he headlined in Rome, Milan, Barcelona, Madrid, London, and New York within just three years of his debut. Following the death of Enrico Caruso, he became one of the brightest stars in the Metropolitan's firmament. Thanks to his brick-built technique, his repertoire was extremely varied, covering everything from the bel canto roles of Bellini's Arturo (*I Puritani*) via the Verdi *spinto* territory (*Luisa Miller*, *Il trovatore*, *Rigoletto*, and *Aida*) to the dramatic roles of Otello (Verdi) and Calaf (Puccini's *Turandot*)—of which he was the first American exponent in 1926.

The voice was bright and ardent, but in almost every performance he determined to reassert himself as ruler of the high Cs, even if none was written into the score. His gluttonous use of portamento was excessive even when portamento was still in fashion, and his quick vibrato infuriated his critics, for whom the broader tone employed by Caruso was the ideal. But Lauri-Volpi could get away with it because he was consistently exciting and periodically capable of great tenderness.

In 1933, having given 232 performances at the Met, he was asked, as was the entire company, to take a pay cut in order to see the house through the Depression. He was one of only two singers—the other being Beniamino Gigli—to refuse. He left New York, with Gigli, and returned to Italy, where he threw his support behind Mussolini and the Fascists. He traveled the country singing at military and political functions until, with the Allied forces advancing over the Italian border, he fled into Spain.

Lauri-Volpi's postwar career never recovered from his political associations, although he continued to perform and was revered by the younger generation. He gave his last staged performances in 1959, although he performed "Nessun dorma" (Puccini's *Turandot*) at a gala in Barcelona in 1972, aged 80, and recorded a disc of arias the following year. He wrote extensively throughout his long life, including numerous books, one of which, *Mysteries of the Human Voice*, is among the most perceptive ever written about singing.

Lauri-Volpi was the unchallenged peacock of American opera during the 1920s and early 1930s, before his refusal to accept a pay cut at the New York Metropolitan Opera forced him to return to Italy.

Lotte
LEHMANN

1 8 8 8 – 1 9 7 6

NO OTHER SINGER of the 20th century so completely possessed a role as German-born American soprano Lotte Lehmann did the role of the Marschallin (Richard Strauss's *Der Rosenkavalier*). Her association with the opera was much admired by Strauss, with whom she was good friends from 1916. That year she moved to the Vienna Hofoper and created the role of the Composer at the first performance of Strauss's revised *Ariadne auf Naxos*.

Her association with the role of the Marschallin and Vienna was, thereafter, central to her reputation as one of the finest lyric-dramatic sopranos of the century. Her status was frequently reinforced by Strauss, who was so taken by the charm and warmth of her voice, and so wholly seduced by her impulsive, irresistibly feminine nature, that he created roles for her such as the Dyer's Wife (*Die Frau ohne Schatten*) and Christine (*Intermezzo*), the model for which was his own wife, the soprano Pauline de Ahna.

It was Strauss who gave Lehmann her first significant opportunity, in 1916. He and the conductor Franz Schalk had wanted Marie Gutheil-Schoder to sing the Composer, but when she failed to turn up at rehearsals, the administrator at the Hofoper, Hans Gregor, suggested Lehmann as her replacement. Strauss agreed to listen to her rehearse, and on the strength of a few minutes' singing, assigned her the role, and overnight celebrity. Gutheil-Schoder never forgave Strauss, and Lehmann never looked back. She went on to sing another Strauss role, Arabella, but thereafter restricted herself to those operas in which she felt at ease, both musically and dramatically.

It would have been inconceivable for her to sing Strauss's Salome or Elektra, and although her voice and personality suited only a limited range of works, she was the master of everything to which she applied herself. She was not comfortable, for example, with Puccini's operas, and yet she was, according to the composer, one of the finest Suor Angelicas (*Suor Angelica*) he had ever seen. Similarly, she was reluctant to sing in anything but German, but her Italian-language Desdemona (Verdi's *Otello*) was thought to rank among the finest ever seen at Covent Garden.

As she was the first to admit, her perfectionism dissuaded her from tackling areas of the repertoire in which she felt vulnerable. Consequently, she devoted herself to the Austro-German operas of Strauss, Mozart, and Wagner. As the latter's Elsa (*Lohengrin*), Eva (*Die Meistersinger*), and Sieglinde (*Die Walküre*), she was peerless, bringing an effortless beauty to the music that many feel has never been equaled. Similarly, her portrayal of Leonora (Beethoven's *Fidelio*) is still spoken of in terms of absolute perfection. Ultimately, for all her achievements as an opera and lieder singer, Lehmann's name will forever be associated with *Der Rosenkavalier* and the Marschallin. A soaring, tragic, beautiful, dignified, and exquisitely diverse creation, it was one of the miracles of the 20th century.

Lehmann was one of Richard Strauss's favorite singers. This typically moody, expressionist portrait was taken in 1933, the year in which she left Nazi Germany, and Strauss's patronage, for the United States.

Lotte
LENYA

1 8 9 8 – 1 9 8 1

AUSTRIAN-BORN AMERICAN singing actress Lotte Lenya will be known to most people as Rosa Klebb, the assassin with a switchblade in the toe of her shoe from the Bond film *From Russia with Love* (1963). However, long before she felt it necessary to stoop to such eccentric amusements, Lenya was one of the 20th century's most influential singing actresses. As the wife, from 1926, of the German-born composer Kurt Weill, she developed and mastered a style of singing that was as contemporary as her husband's music.

Lenya took much of her inspiration from her experiences at the Berlin Schauspielhaus, where German playwright Frank Wedekind's experiments with cabaret, his anticipation of the Theater of the Absurd, and his declamatory style of ballad singing greatly influenced Lenya's work as a performer. In 1927 Lenya accompanied Weill to the Baden-Baden festival of modern music, where she sang one of the two female leads in the premiere of Weill and German playwright Bertolt Brecht's cantata *Mahagonny*. The following year she achieved international acclaim for her performance as Jenny in the premiere of Weill's *Die Dreigroschenoper* (*The Threepenny Opera*) in Berlin.

Somewhere between singing and speaking, Lenya's vocal technique was defined first and foremost by the culture that formed it, so that even when performing one of Weill's supine melodies, there was always a hint of the drawling, cabaret-infused style she learned from Wedekind. Weill made much of this instantly recognizable quality in three further works—the "spectacle" *Die sieben Todsünden* (1933), *The Eternal Road*, a bibilical drama (1937), and the operetta *The Firebrand of Florence* (1944).

At the time of Weill's death in 1950, Lenya was among the best-known performers of her generation. She devoted her remaining years to the revival and performance of Weill's music, particularly his "lost" German works, composed before their exile to the United States in 1935 (they had been forced to leave Germany after the rise of Nazism). Eventually, Lenya's unique style of vocalization was recognized as "classical," and the likes of Ute Lemper have sustained a tradition that might well have died out with Lenya had it not been for her rehabilitation of Weill's operas.

Lenya was a uniquely charismatic and inventive performer. She had a superb ear for character and was an actress of acute invention and intuition. Her cool approach to performance gave her a reputation for detachment, which was largely unwarranted since she was an extremely passionate woman. She was a highly disciplined and, in certain works, virtuoso performer, and if her style of singing was bound up with the work of one man, then this narrow focus in no way distracts from her significance as an opera singer. There are many styles of opera, and Lenya proved that the singing voice was quite as open to reinvention as the medium in which she and Weill scored so many memorable successes.

One need only think of Lenya's barbed-wire voice to imagine her in performance, and no photograph better emphasizes her dramatic qualities than this shot of her in concert, performing Weill's cabaret songs.

George
LONDON

1919–1985

WHEN THE GERMAN conductor Hans Knappertsbusch was first introduced to the Canadian baritone George London in Bayreuth in 1951, he turned to Wieland Wagner, the composer's grandson, and announced, "If his singing is as good as his looks, then we'll be all right." It was, and they were. London's performances as Amfortas in the 1951 *Parsifal* (Wagner) assured him a celebrity in Europe commensurate with his standing in the United States. There he was known to millions through his performances alongside Frances Yeend and Mario Lanza as one third of the erroneously titled Bel Canto Trio.

From 1947 the trio toured for two seasons, scoring huge successes on the radio and in concert but never in the theater. At the end of 1948 London left the United States for Vienna and a fortuitous audition with the Austrian conductor Karl Böhm. So impressed was Böhm that he immediately signed him to the company of the Vienna Staatsoper, where he made his European debut as Amonasro (Verdi's *Aida*) in 1949. Word spread of London's exceptionally large and dark baritone, and within two years he had sung Figaro (Mozart) at Glyndebourne, Pizarro (Beethoven's *Fidelio*) at La Scala, Amonasro at the Metropolitan in New York, and the aforementioned Amfortas at Bayreuth in 1951.

While London's progress was meteoric, it was predominantly European. However, he enjoyed many triumphs in the United States, notable among them being his portrayal of Mandryka at the Metropolitan premiere of *Arabella* (Richard Strauss) in 1956—a role he reprised for the first studio recording of the opera two years later—and as Abdul in the first production at the Met of *The Last Savage* (Menotti). He gave his greatest performances in Russia, Italy, Germany, and Austria, particularly the latter two, where he was generally thought to be the greatest Wotan (Wagner's *Der Ring*) after Hans Hotter. His prestige in Vienna was augmented by further successes in productions of *Eugene Onegin* (Tchaikovsky) and *Les contes d'Hoffmann* (Offenbach), and by his reputation as the first American to sing Mozart in Salzburg, the first American to sing the Dutchman (Wagner's *Der fliegende Holländer*) in Bayreuth, and, in 1960, the first American to sing Boris Godounov (Mussorgsky) at the Bolshoi Theater, a portrayal that survives on a memorable recording.

After his singing career was cut short in 1967 by the paralysis of one of his vocal cords, London worked as a producer and was appointed director of various arts institutions, including Washington Opera, before finally retiring after a heart ailment was diagnosed in 1979. After his death six years later, the Swedish soprano Birgit Nilsson, who partnered him regularly in Wagner operas, recalled how: "In the many performances I have appeared in, there were many wonderful colleagues who had me in raptures. There were those with magnificent voices or [who were] great musicians, wonderful actors or great personalities. But George London had it all!"

Even without his enormous voice, London's physically overwhelming appearance would have been sufficient to carry him through his favored repertoire of Wagner and Richard Strauss.

93

Giovanni
MARTINELLI

1 8 8 5 – 1 9 6 9

IN 1913, AS THE curtain fell on a performance of *La bohème* (Puccini) at Covent Garden, in which Italian tenor Giovanni Martinelli had sung Rodolfo to Nellie Melba's Mimi, the diva marched to the footlights to acknowledge what she thought to be the audience's cries of "Aunty Nellie! Aunty Nellie!" When it was diplomatically pointed out to Melba that the audience was actually chanting "Martinelli! Martinelli!," the ever-modest tenor was persuaded to step forward and acknowledge the applause as his own.

The story rings true. Aside from Enrico Caruso, no other 20th-century tenor was so wholly loved by his public. His sincere and unpretentious approach to what he considered to be the artless science of singing, nourished by an unusually warm personality and professional generosity, brought him international acclaim and respect during a career that spanned nearly half a century of performances. Among them were 30 uninterrupted years as the New York Metropolitan's leading dramatic tenor and hundreds of recordings, as well as the devotion of almost every conductor and composer with whom he worked, including Toscanini and Puccini. It is only through an appreciation of Martinelli's human qualities that his standing as one of the century's greatest singers can be understood, for his was one of the least attractive voices ever to warrant the flattery of universal acclaim.

As tenors go, it was an inborn, untutored instrument. The voice was raw and uneven in its placing, with an arrant use of portamento passing for phrasing. For most of his career, he used little or no vibrato and he employed a conspicuously slim range of expressive color. The tone of the voice could veer in a single phrase between tooth-rattling splendor and ear-splitting howling, and even in his prime, during the 1920s, Martinelli was prone to sing woefully out of tune.

For all that, he was hugely popular. His popularity is partly explained by the fact that, given the right circumstances and a felicitous role, he was capable of generating an almost carnal sense of excitement among an audience. As Manrico (Verdi's *Il trovatore*), Andrea Chénier (Giordano), Cavaradossi (Puccini's *Tosca*), Alvaro (Verdi's *La forza del destino*), Canio (Leoncavallo's *Pagliacci*), and Dick Johnson (Puccini's *La fanciulla del West*), he was magnificent. But it was as Calaf (Puccini's *Turandot*) and Otello (Verdi) that he was pre-eminent. As the latter he was without rival during the 1930s, as a live recording from the Metropolitan testifies, and it is a measure of his stamina that he was able to carry on singing the role until 1947. However, most of those live performances to have survived from the 1940s demonstrate how fragile the voice was in its maturity. That his career continued despite such painfully obvious deterioration can be explained only as a consequence of his natural dramatic flair and popular standing.

A hugely engaging and likable artist, Martinelli sang a huge number of roles, some of which, such as the Duke of Mantua in Verdi's Rigoletto *(as whom he is pictured here), were completely unsuited to his talents. Regardless, he was a star whatever the opera he performed in.*

Victor
MAUREL

1 8 4 8 – 1 9 2 3

NINETEENTH-CENTURY ITALIANS were known for their pride. If a foreigner found himself competing for a job that a native could do less well, then the native invariably got the job, and nowhere was this bias more overt than in the opera house. It was a measure of a foreign singer's talents if he or she managed to win the affections of the Italian public, since he or she must already have won over an assembly of impresarios, conductors, and composers. One of the most successful, and remarkable, foreign singers of the Italian late 19th century was the French baritone Victor Maurel.

Maurel was one of the most influential performers of his day, and a major force in the transformation of opera singers into singing actors. He made his debut in 1867, performing throughout France in much the same repertoire as his rival, Jean-Baptiste Faure. When it became obvious that Faure had established something of a monopoly in Paris, Maurel tried his luck in foreign parts. After successful performances in St. Petersburg, Cairo, and Venice, he made his way, in 1870, to Milan, and La Scala, where he was picked from relative obscurity to create the role of Gonzales in Carlos Gomes' *Il Guarany*. The huge success of the opera reflected well on Maurel, bringing him to the attention of Verdi and securing him a central position in the La Scala company. He remained in Milan until 1879, when he returned to Paris, and his rightful place as the principal baritone at the Opéra.

In 1881 Verdi summoned Maurel to create the title role in the first production of the revised *Simon Boccanegra*. His performance so impressed the composer that when, in 1884, Verdi began work on the score of *Otello*, he conceived the role of Iago for Maurel's unique talents. The premiere three years later was a complete triumph, and no one was greatly surprised when, in 1893, it emerged that Verdi had asked Maurel to create the title role in *Falstaff*, his transcription of Shakespeare's *The Merry Wives of Windsor*. By this time Maurel was an "honorary" Italian, and no one begrudged his preeminence since it was obvious to just about everyone that he was the best man for the job. This much was recognized a year earlier by a little-known composer called Leoncavallo, who asked Maurel to create the role of Tonio in the first performance of his latest opera, *Pagliacci*.

Maurel was one of the first true singing actors. His voice was neither large nor particularly rich, but its range of expressive color was so great and his declamatory powers so intense that he was able to bring to life even the weakest doggerel. Lilli Lehmann, for example, recalled how after witnessing Maurel as Valentin in a performance of Gounod's *Faust*, she was left "speechless for hours."

Maurel was a legend long before his death, and to know that he was as good as his reputation, one need look no further than Verdi's confidence and the extraordinary affection and respect that he commanded as a Frenchman in foreign lands.

Maurel was Verdi's first Iago and his first Falstaff—as whom he is pictured here—and the "ideal," according to the composer, for most of his baritone roles.

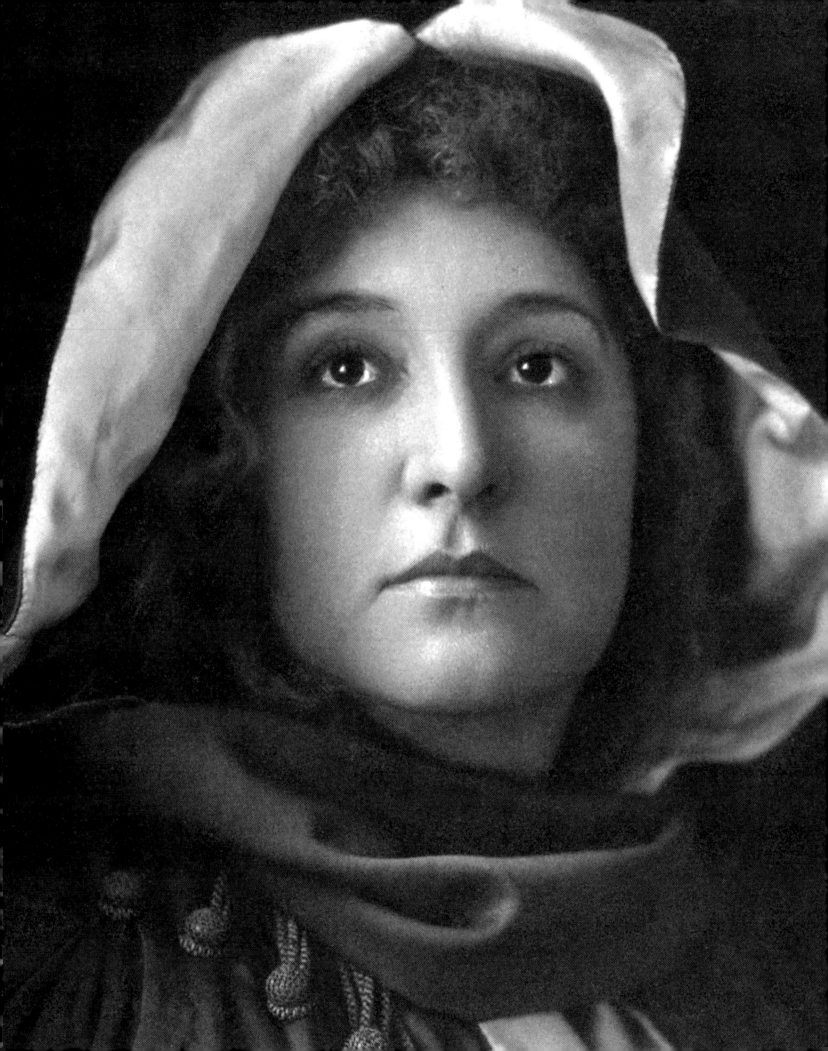

Nellie
MELBA

1861–1931

IF THE AUSTRALIAN soprano Nellie Melba had never existed, someone would have imagined her. She was, and for many people remains, the archetype of the operatic diva: petulant, selfish, august, glamorous, and brilliant. Her life off the stage was as much a subject for discussion, gossip, and reportage as her work on it, and even when her voice had begun to fray around the edges, she continued to draw an unparalleled concentration of attention and affection.

Born Helen Mitchell, Melba changed her name out of respect for her birthplace, Melbourne, but felt compelled to refine her craft in Europe, and in 1886 she left for Paris and a year's study with Mathilde Marchesi. She made her debut in Brussels in 1887, and during the next 10 years she perfected her technique to become the most gifted coloratura soprano of her day. In 1890 she turned to the lyric repertoire, scoring huge successes in Paris and London as Juliette (Gounod's *Roméo et Juliette*) and Marguerite (Gounod's *Faust*)—roles she had studied with the composer.

Between 1892 and 1894 she triumphed at La Scala as Gilda (Verdi's *Rigoletto*) and Lucia (Donizetti's *Lucia di Lammermoor*), and in 1893 she began a 17-year association with the New York Metropolitan. This was famously interrupted in 1907 when Oscar Hammerstein offered her such obscene sums of money that she agreed to join his Manhattan Opera House. In the run-up to her first performance of *La traviata* (Verdi) for Hammerstein, the newspapers turned over unconscionable column space to everything from Melba's costumes and her $2.5 million collection of jewelry to her infamous control compulsion. But it was for her singing that audiences turned up, and after the first night one critic reported: "The enthusiasm of the audience passed all bounds, and for some minutes there was a deafening uproar…"

She was no less an institution in London, where audiences at Covent Garden revered her as something of a deity. At her farewell to Covent Garden in 1926—which survives on record—most of the effusive tributes were interrupted by weeping, spontaneous acclamations, and some of the finest singing the house had ever heard.

Melba was a diva in the best and worse senses of the word. She ruled, on and off the stage, with an iron hand in an iron glove. The voice was small but exquisitely beautiful, with a glorious floated upper register, a full and even tone, and one of the most perfect legatos ever heard. Technically, there was little beyond her, and her trills, scales, and runs set an almost unreachable standard. Austere though she may have been, Melba was a grand character in a grand tradition and quite aware of the absurdity of her situation. When she was informed by an American journalist that she was earning more money than the president, she replied, "Then the silly man should learn to sing!"

Melba may now be remembered as the progenitor of a sweet dessert, but in her prime she was the measure of operatic celebrity and the very model for all aspiring prima donnas.

Lauritz
MELCHIOR

1 8 9 0 – 1 9 7 3

HAD IT NOT been for the Danish tenor Lauritz Melchior, the Wagner tenor might still be thought of in the same terms as the mythical love of *Tristan und Isolde*—as an ideal to be aspired to but never attained. So demanding are the roles of Tristan (*Tristan und Isolde*), Siegmund (*Die Walküre*), Siegfried, and Parsifal that Wagner himself accepted that few singers would ever be able to surmount their physical, vocal, and interpretative demands. But Melchior proved to the world that Wagner's musical imagination had been founded entirely on the possible, and his remarkable achievements during the 1920s, 1930s, and 1940s, as the Wagner tenor par excellence, established a benchmark against which every subsequent generation has measured its expectations.

Melchior was born in Copenhagen, Denmark, on exactly the same day (March 20) as one of the world's other great tenors, Beniamino Gigli. Melchior began his career in 1913 as a high baritone but moved up a register five years later. He studied in Berlin, Munich, and London—where he made his debut in 1924—and later that same year he was heard for the first time at Bayreuth. Such was the joy there that even Wagner's reclusive widow, Cosima, was persuaded to attend rehearsals for Melchior's debut as Siegfried.

The giant Dane had his rivals—notably Max Lorenz, Ludwig Suthaus, and Set Svanholm—and each was thought of as Melchior's superior as an actor but none was so prodigiously gifted with the necessary vocal attributes of a Wagner tenor. The baritonal weight of sound, evenness of placement, and ringing high notes gave him a vocal security that enabled him to dominate even the most frenzied of Wagner's orchestrations. For the first time in living memory, Melchior demonstrated how a tenor might successfully apply himself to more than just the mechanics of endurance.

Ironically, his stamina proved an irritation to some, primarily those for whom the course of a singer's inevitable fatigue carried within it a reflection of a character's journey through an opera, but few were able to deny the real pleasure of hearing the closing duet of *Siegfried* or the final act of *Tristan* sung with such heroic, unfaded vitality.

Such was his technique, and so great his physical strength, that Melchior was able to continue singing in superb voice until the year of his death, when he was recorded, in stereo, giving a remarkably fresh performance of the final scene of the first act of *Die Walküre*. Even in his 83rd year he was better equipped to tackle the role of Siegmund than most of his younger colleagues. Marvel as we do at Melchior's superhuman strength and tireless voice, he cast a long and ultimately suffocating shadow. More than a century after his birth, each new Wagner tenor is forced to contend with the great Dane's legacy, and had it not been for his defining contribution to the history of German opera, we might not today be asking where all the tenors have gone.

Melchior in later years, after his retirement from the stage, was in much the same sort of form as he had been in his youth, when his emotional exuberance and physical size made his performances uniquely thrilling.

Robert
MERRILL

b. 1917

ALTHOUGH THE TRADITIONS of the Jewish cantor helped establish the synagogue as a nursery for fine singing, remarkably few American Jews found their way into American opera houses. Of those who did, arguably the best known, and certainly one of the most talented, was baritone Moishe Miller—otherwise known as Robert Merrill.

Like many other American children born to early 20th-century Jewish immigrants, Merrill aspired to his host culture, and for much of his childhood, he yearned for fame and glory as a baseball star. His mother, a concert singer, had other ideas and was determined to see him relinquish the pitching mound of the New York Yankees for the stage of the city's Metropolitan Opera. After years of grudging study, Merrill eventually yielded to his mother's persistence when he began to discover what would eventually mature into one of the 20th century's most glorious baritone voices. But before Merrill triumphed on the operatic stage, he achieved national celebrity through his performances on the radio, not least through his own show and a regular spot at the Radio City Music Hall.

In 1944, buoyed by his celebrity, Merrill waltzed into the Met for an audition, roared his way through "Largo al factotum," and winced as a voice from the stalls called out, "Next." Having been brought crashing down to earth, he returned to study and managed to find his way into staged performances of *Aida* (Verdi) and *Carmen* (Bizet). He returned to the Met in 1945 for his second audition and this time walked off with the first prize and a contract. Later that year he was chosen by conductor Arturo Toscanini to sing the role of Germont (Verdi's *La traviata*) on his RCA recording with American soprano Licia Albanese and American tenor Jan Peerce. The honor was repeated in 1954 when Toscanini invited him to sing Renato on his recording of *Un ballo in maschera* (Verdi), but not until the 1950/1951 season did he headline a production—as Posa in *Don Carlos* (Verdi).

Only a few weeks later, Merrill was fired for "breach of contract," having accepted an offer to appear in a film, *Aaron Slick from Pumpkin Crick*. After the film bombed, he successfully persuaded the Met's manager, Rudolf Bing, to allow him back in 1952, and thereafter Merrill reigned supreme as the Met's principal baritone. He gave more than 1,000 performances of an astonishing 85 roles, among which his Rigoletto (Verdi), Scarpia (Puccini's *Tosca*), and Figaro (Rossini's *Il barbiere di Siviglia*) were vocally beyond compare.

Merrill was a true celebrity, in that while he was first and foremost an opera singer, he also wanted to be an entertainer of as many people from as many walks of life as possible. He would, therefore, work with just about anyone, including the likes of Frank Sinatra and Louis Armstrong. He also continued to perform on the radio and television, and between 1970 and 1974 he gave some 500 performances as Tevje in the Broadway production of Jerry Bock and Sheldon Harnick's *Fiddler on the Roof*.

Merrill was one of the great virtuosos of American opera and a mentor to New York's Jewish community, for whom he was, during his prime, something of an idol.

Sherrill
MILNES

b. 1935

THE TRADITION OF the American über-baritone, as embodied by the likes of Lawrence Tibbett, Robert Merrill, and Leonard Warren, has always favored vocal skill above dramatic concentration, but Sherrill Milnes took this imbalance to its natural conclusion and built an international career on the performance of opera as oratorio. His capacity for hair-raising displays of vocal prowess at the expense of any real sense of character or temperament made him an ideal recording artist, and after Dietrich Fischer-Dieskau he is probably the most prolific operatic baritone of the 20th century.

His self-consciously handsome presence and one-dimensional approach to stage-craft—whereby every role, whether hero or villain, enjoyed the same weight and color of interpretation—have in no way hindered his career. While he symbolizes that peculiar breed of opera star for whom the brilliance of the surface served to distract from the almost total lack of substance, he was, at his best, unrivaled in the dramatic repertoire on which his reputation was founded.

A career as an opera singer must have seemed a very distant prospect during his childhood on a dairy farm in Downers Grove, Illinois. His parents encouraged his obvious musical talents, arranging for lessons on the piano, clarinet, the whole quartet of stringed instruments, and tuba, but Milnes always took the greatest pleasure from his voice. After high school, music lost out to medical studies, but in 1960 he joined the Boris Goldovsky Opera Company, making his debut as Masetto in *Don Giovanni* (Mozart) that year. Just four years later he joined the New York City Opera as Valentin (Gounod's *Faust*), in which role he made his Metropolitan Opera debut the same year.

Almost from the outset, critics and colleagues alike were struck by the enormous power and range of Milnes' voice. The huge reach, which took him well into the tenor register, effortless legato, and articulate diction made him an ideal all-purpose baritone, but he quickly became associated with Verdi, as whose Miller (*Luisa Miller*) he leaped to international celebrity at the Met in 1968. In his roles as Verdi's Macbeth, Rigoletto, di Luna (*Il trovatore*), Riccardo (*Un ballo in maschera*), Carlo (*La forza del destino*), and Iago (*Otello*), all of which he has recorded to great effect, he was vocally magnificent, if a little mechanical. But he was unequivocally outstanding in the blunter, less subtle regions of the *verismo* repertoire, chiefly as Escamillo (Bizet's *Carmen*), Tonio (Leoncavallo's *Pagliacci*), Gérard (Giordano's *Andrea Chénier*), and Jack Rance (Puccini's *La fanciulla del West*).

Although his voice declined in the late 1980s, Milnes has continued to perform into his sixties, adding new roles to his enormous repertoire. But he was at his best during the 1970s and early 1980s when, alongside Luciano Pavarotti and Joan Sutherland, he was part of one of the most remarkable repertoire trios in the history of opera.

Physically imposing and vocally magisterial, Milnes was a formidable operatic villain—not least as Iago (Verdi's Otello), as he is pictured here, to Domingo's Otello.

Birgit
NILSSON

b. 1918

THE HISTORY OF opera has nothing to compare with Swedish soprano Birgit Nilsson. As the most complete dramatic soprano of the 20th century, she stood outside the normal parameters of analysis and assessment. She consistently defied all and any comparisons as—with the exception of Norwegian soprano Kirsten Flagstad—there was no precedent for, and no rival to, her unique blend of talents, and she is alone in having achieved the formidable feat of pleasing all of the people all of the time.

Amid an art form doomed to the abuse of absolutes, Nilsson really was the greatest dramatic soprano of them all. Her invulnerable technique, intuitive artistry, and the sheer majesty of the voice set her apart in almost everything she did, so that even her immediate rivals, some of them bitterly competitive, acceded to her primacy as Isolde (Wagner's *Tristan und Isolde*), Brünnhilde (Wagner's *Der Ring*), Sieglinde (Wagner's *Die Walküre*), Salome (Richard Strauss), Elektra (Strauss), and Turandot (Puccini).

Born in West Karup, Sweden, Nilsson was a late starter, entering the Stockholm Royal Academy in 1941. She made her debut at the Royal Opera in 1946, aged 28, as Agathe in Weber's *Der Freischütz*. It was quickly realized that her voice was perhaps a size too large for the early romantic repertoire, and the following year she created a sensation as Lady Macbeth (Verdi's *Macbeth*) in a production conducted by Fritz Busch.

There followed many of the roles that she was later to make her own, such as Sieglinde (Wagner's *Die Walküre*), Venus (Wagner's *Tannhäuser*), Senta (Wagner's *Der fliegende Holländer*), and Aida (Verdi), but it was not until 1954 that Nilsson achieved international celebrity. Performing Salome in Stockholm, Brünnhilde in Munich, and a variety of roles in Vienna and Bayreuth, she was hailed for the enormous power of her voice, the intelligence of her portrayals, and her tireless stamina, attributes that marked her out as the finest Wagner soprano of her generation. In this capacity she reigned unchallenged for the next 30 years, scoring successive triumphs on the world's most prestigious stages, including a run at Bayreuth that spanned from 1953 to 1970.

The voice was a bundle of paradoxes: it was penetrating yet responsive, enormous but flexible, imperious yet tender, herculean but always human. The only area of repertoire in which she was perhaps less than ideal was early Strauss. That said, such was the heroic quality of her singing, and the sheer opulence of the instrument, that few really cared, and even when performing those areas of Italian repertoire for which she was less than ideal (such as Verdi's Amelia in *Un ballo in maschera*), Nilsson's vocal majesty more than compensated for the uncertain diction and idiomatic stylization. The greatest Isolde and Brünnhilde of the century, Nilsson set new standards for the dramatic soprano, and her performances will doubtless remain the ideal against which all others are measured.

Nilsson was not a large woman, yet she possessed one of the grandest voices of the 20th century, which she used to remarkable effect in the operas of Wagner and Richard Strauss.

Jessye
NORMAN

b. 1945

As demonstrated by Kathleen Battle's experiences at the New York Metropolitan Opera, the diva is today something of a dinosaur. But not all the dinosaurs died out at once, and there remains a handful of operatic stars whose talent, self-confidence, and commercial influence are sufficient to allow them an almost regal dispensation to dictate who, what, when, and where. At the top of this thinning tree sits American soprano Jessye Norman, a singer of rare ability and the godmother of the American operatic scene.

Her famously precious attitude to her art has created its own mythology. Even now stories circulate of her contractual demands, which are said to stipulate everything from the temperature of her dressing-rooms to her eye-popping fees, huge entourage, and dietary requirements. There is no smoke without fire—and her infamously litigious attitude to the press has quashed most of the more eccentric rumors—but she is a great deal less precious than many like to think. Ultimately, as one impresario admitted, even the most unorthodox peccadillo pales into insignificance once the great lady begins to sing.

Born in Augusta, Georgia, Norman began singing in church soon after her fourth birthday. Her musical talent was encouraged through to university, where she began to master her leviathan soprano voice. She made her debut in Berlin in 1969, as Elisabeth in *Tannhäuser* (Wagner). While choosing not to specialize as a Wagner soprano (embracing everything from Haydn, Gluck, and Mozart to Strauss, Stravinsky, and Schoenberg), it was to the German romantic repertory that her talents leant themselves.

As Leonore (Beethoven's *Fidelio*), Euryanthe (Weber's *Euryanthe*), and Agathe (Weber's *Der Freischütz*), to say nothing of Elsa (Wagner's *Lohengrin*), Sieglinde (Wagner's *Die Walküre*), and Kundry (Wagner's *Parsifal*), she was without serious rival. Ironically, while the range and power of her voice would seem tailor-made for the bench-pressing role of Salome (Richard Strauss), her performances (and recording in 1995) as the dangerous teenager demonstrated, once and for all, that Strauss was after less, not more, when it came to matters of characterization and inflection.

Norman's soprano is enormous, even in cavernous venues such as the Met, but she can wield it with exceptional delicacy and sensuality. If it lacks the edge characteristic of her Nordic colleagues, then its essential warmth and beauty enable her to project an unusual variety of expression and personality—sufficient for her to excel as a lieder recitalist as well as a *dramatischer Sopran*.

If critics and opera-lovers are divided as to her merits as an actress, then there are few sopranos capable of so consistently meeting the vocal demands of some of the most difficult roles in opera. It remains to be seen if, in the twilight of her career, she will decide to sing the sanctified role of Isolde (Wagner's *Tristan und Isolde*).

One of Norman's most memorable performances at the Met was in the title role of Strauss's Ariadne auf Naxos. *Here she recreates the role at Covent Garden in 1985.*

Adelina
PATTI

1843–1919

IN HIS MEMOIRS the impresario Henry Mapleson recalled of Italian soprano Adelina Patti that she was "beyond doubt the most successful singer who ever lived." Even though she was among the best-known and most talented sopranos of her day—a very long day that extended from her performing debut as a seven-year-old in 1850 to her conclusive retirement 64 years later—Patti's celebrity owed as much to her extraordinary eccentricities, lifestyle, and wealth as it did to her talents as a singer.

After 1882 she demanded, and received, a minimum of $5,000 (about $160,000 in today's money) for each single performance, refused to attend any rehearsals, made contractual stipulations about the size of the lettering on posters carrying her name, and insisted, when touring the United States, that her collection of jewels—valued in terms of millions of dollars—be chaperoned by three armed guards wherever she went.

Sadly, the ephemera surrounding her career have obscured the truth of her talent, which was a great deal more remarkable than her lifestyle. The daughter of two celebrated singers, Patti was a prodigy of Mozartian proportions. Her singing voice reached its first maturity in her seventh year, when her ear was so perfect that she could instantly repeat and remember whatever was played to her. She was also able, without training or tuition, to surmount technical challenges that normally required years of study.

The precocious infant matured into an exceptional adult, prized and adored by colleagues and public alike. Rossini, who made changes to the role of Rosina in *Il barbiere di Siviglia* especially for her, Gounod, and Verdi, who declared her the greatest singer he had ever heard, were all devoted admirers of her artistry. Although her reputation was founded on the bel canto repertoire, and the operas of Rossini, Donizetti, and Bellini, she was very much a patron of what was then contemporary music, performing in operas by Bizet, Meyerbeer, Thomas, and Verdi.

Patti's pure, sweet soprano and dazzling technique seduced all who heard it. The voice was small but remarkable for its wide range, evenness of production, and purity of tone. She was without doubt the supreme exponent of coloratura, and although in later years she was a singer first and an actress never, she was a notable dramatist during her prime, between 1863 and 1880, when she achieved legendary successes in comedy as well as tragedy. Although she officially retired in 1906, she continued to sing into her seventies, making a series of 78 rpms for HMV at her castle, Craig-y-Nos, in Wales. These recordings amply demonstrate what it was that made her such a legend. Moreover they provide a glimpse into history, since they capture the singing voice of a woman admired by some of the greatest, most influential composers of the 19th century, not least her friend Rossini, who was born in 1792 and at whose funeral she sang in 1868.

Patti was the quintessential prima donna. To great physical discomfort, and with complete disregard for her diaphragm, she would wear whalebone corsets, such as the one she is wearing here, while performing on stage.

Luciano
PAVAROTTI

b. 1935

ITALIAN TENOR LUCIANO Pavarotti's 1961 debut, as Rodolfo (Puccini's *La bohème*) in Reggio Emilia, is one of those events in the history of opera at which there must have been an audience of 10,000, so many are those who claim to have been there. This celebrated event was recorded, so it is possible to hear the gasps of astonishment that greeted the tenor's heart-stopping high C at the close of Rodolfo's first-act aria. If the audience was unappreciative of how huge Pavarotti would one day become, then it was instantly aware of the rarity of his talent. Like the millions who have since marveled at Pavarotti's performances on record and television, the spectators were united in their appreciation of what was quite plainly one of the most perfect lyric tenors of all time.

Pavarotti's throat was truly kissed by God. No other tenor in the last 100 years has benefited from such a wholly natural and instinctive vocal dexterity, and it is to his credit that neither he nor his tutors interfered with the elemental naiveté of the instrument. Pavarotti had no need for a vocal method, since his voice was born fully formed. Although he effectively ruined it through poor repertoire decisions, between the early 1960s and the late 1970s, he was unrivaled in the bel canto repertoire.

Two years after his debut in Reggio Emilia, Pavarotti substituted for Giuseppe di Stefano at Covent Garden, again as Rodolfo, and in 1964 he was invited to Glyndebourne, where he sang Idamantes (Mozart's *Idomeneo*). The following year he toured Australia with Joan Sutherland as Edgardo to her Lucia (Donizetti's *Lucia di Lammermoor*), the success of which led to his debut at La Scala as the Duke of Mantua (Verdi's *Rigoletto*) in 1965. In 1968 he appeared in San Francisco, as Edgardo and Tonio (Donizetti's *La fille du régiment*), where his performances secured him a place at the New York Met.

In the operas of Bellini, Donizetti, and early Verdi, Pavarotti was without rival, pouring an irresistible warmth of soul and voice into some of the most gloriously generous, effortlessly phrased, and poignantly expressive performances ever witnessed on an operatic stage. His endless ringing high notes were a thing of legend. In particular, his famously witty and charming portrayal of Tonio saw, for the first time in half a century, a tenor capable of waltzing through the fearsome assault course of "Ah, mes amis," a sensational showpiece that ends with nine consecutive high Cs.

During the 1970s Pavarotti began to perform much darker, more dramatic roles. With Decca's encouragement, he performed and recorded a huge swathe of repertoire for which he was vocally, temperamentally, and dramatically ill equipped. Long before the onset of global celebrity during the late 1980s, aided by his part in the Three Tenors' carnival, Pavarotti was some way past his best. His work since added insult to injury for those among his fans who remembered what it was that made him famous in the first place.

Pavarotti in costume as the Duke of Mantua (Verdi's Rigoletto*), atop a hill at his Po River Valley birthplace in Italy. This was the role in which he made his La Scala debut in 1965.*

Peter
PEARS

1910–1986

IT WAS ONCE the case that every composer created each new role with the particular
talents of a specific singer in mind. The last such notable collaboration, and certainly one
of the most creative, was that between the English tenor Peter Pears and English composer Benjamin Britten. They first met in 1936, when Pears was a member of the New
English Singers and Britten was a little-known composer of concert music. A year later
they began to work together in recital, and in 1939 they left together for the United
States, where Pears encouraged Britten to write his first theatrical work, the operetta *Paul
Bunyan*, for which their friend W. H. Auden wrote the libretto.

They returned to England in 1942, as partners as well as colleagues, and Pears made
his stage debut at the Strand Theatre, as Hoffmann (Offenbach's *Les contes d'Hoffmann*).
In 1943 he joined Sadler's Wells, working his way through the popular light-tenor repertoire, including Almaviva (Rossini's *Il barbiere di Siviglia*), Rodolfo (Puccini's *La bohème*),
and—in a particularly celebrated interpretation—Vasek (Smetana's *The Bartered Bride*).

On June 7, 1945, Pears created the title role in the premiere, at Sadler's Wells, of
Britten's first full-scale opera, *Peter Grimes*. The success and impact of this work confirmed Britten's genius as a dramatist, and Pears' talent as an interpreter, and for the next
30 years, until Britten's death in 1976, they lived and worked together in what was almost
certainly the most productive composer–performer pairing since before the 19th century.

In 1946, buoyed by the success of *Grimes*, they founded the English Opera Group,
with which Pears created the role of the Male Chorus in Britten's *The Rape of Lucretia*
(1946) and the title role in *Albert Herring* (1947), both at Glyndebourne. In 1951 they
returned to Covent Garden for the premiere of *Billy Budd*, in which Pears sang the role of
Captain Vere. Two years later Covent Garden staged the first performance of *Gloriana*—
which describes the later years of Elizabeth I's reign—and Pears' celebrated creation of
the Earl of Essex. In 1954 they traveled to Venice for the premiere of *The Turn of the
Screw*. Six years later, for the opening of Britten's Jubilee Hall theater in Aldeburgh, Pears
sang the small role of Flute in *A Midsummer Night's Dream*. Between 1964 and 1973,
Britten composed a further six operas: *Curlew River* (1964), *The Burning Fiery Furnace*
(1966), *The Prodigal Son* (1968), *Owen Wingrave* (1971), and *Death in Venice* (1973)—each
of which had been conceived for Pears' outstanding talents as a singing actor.

Pears' voice and artistry were of a rare caliber. The instrument was light but highly
expressive, with an effortlessly English concentration on clarity and diction. His style was
naturally reflective, if not a little insular, but when necessary he was capable of heroics.
For all his many successes, however, his achievements as a performer were dwarfed by the
huge contribution he made to Britten's life and work as a composer.

*Pears triumphed in a huge range of music, in numerous languages, and on many of the world's best-loved stages.
Here he is seen rehearsing in 1962 for the premiere of Britten's* War Requiem *in Coventry Cathedral in England.*

Alfred
PICCAVER

1 8 8 4 – 1 9 5 8

ENGLISH TENOR ALFRED Piccaver is not commonly thought of in terms of operatic iconography, since his celebrity was confined to a single city, Vienna. However, within that city Piccaver exercised a fascination, and earned a reputation, second only to Enrico Caruso. Despite his disinclination (rather than his failure) to globetrot, he was the most celebrated British opera singer in the first half of the 20th century and one of the defining figures in the history of Vienna, Europe's most resonant cultural center.

Piccaver was born in Long Sutton, Lincolnshire, but lived most of his early life in New York, where he won a scholarship in his 21st year to the Opera School of the Metropolitan Opera. In 1907 he was "sent" by his family to Europe and eventually to Vienna, where he entered a regional singing audition. Such was the reaction to his performances that he was engaged by the Prague Opera, where he quickly became the leading box-office attraction. In May 1910 the Italian baritone Mattia Battistini arrived in Prague with his company for performances of *La traviata* (Verdi). When the company's Alfredo fell ill, Piccaver was sent for and so impressed Battistini that he insisted the tenor travel with them to Vienna for their appearances at the Hofoper. Before the end of his first performance, Piccaver was offered a contract by the theater's music director, Felix Weingartner.

In 1912, shortly before his contract in Vienna was to start, Piccaver received a seemingly unrefusable invitation from the New York Metropolitan, which offered to pay him $600 (rising to $800) a night—$7,500 to $10,000 in today's money—for four seasons' work between 1913 and 1917. To general bewilderment, Piccaver turned down the honor, which was never repeated. It was not an unwise decision, for in New York he was doomed to an eternity in Caruso's shadow, whereas in Vienna he was assured absolute primacy, a status that remained unchallenged until the arrival of Swede Jussi Björling in the 1930s.

Ironically, Piccaver's voice was often compared to Caruso's, in that it had weight as well as brightness, smoothness as well as drama. Unlike Caruso, however, Piccaver was a lazy actor, and he made poor use of the words, instead relying on beauty of tone. But as Lotte Lehmann, his regular partner at the Vienna Opera, later recalled, few really cared since "the caressing velvet of his voice was so unbelievably beautiful."

After returning to England to live shortly before Hitler's annexation of Austria in 1938, Piccaver struggled and found himself a stranger in his own land. In 1955 he was invited back to Vienna for the reopening of the Staatsoper, destroyed in 1945 by Allied bombs. He entered the city a hero and never left. At his funeral three years later, thousands of admirers followed his coffin past the front of the opera house. As the procession halted in front of the main entrance, the Vienna Philharmonic Orchestra solemnly played the funeral march from Beethoven's *Eroica*. Not bad for an English lad from Lincolnshire.

Piccaver was revered during his lifetime for his performances in Vienna, where he was greatly admired by Puccini as Cavaradossi (Tosca), as whom he is pictured here.

Ezio
PINZA

1892–1957

NOT SURPRISINGLY, LIFE has rarely imitated art in the necessarily orderly world of opera, but during the 1930s and 1940s, one singer came remarkably close to turning the fantasy into reality for huge numbers of the American public. Despite all evidence to the contrary, it was felt that the similarities between Italian bass Ezio Pinza and his most celebrated creation, Don Giovanni (Mozart), were such that it was impossible to tell the two apart. Tall, elegant, athletic, and breathtakingly handsome, Pinza was also a consummate womanizer, and his amorous exploits sustained an entire generation of New York gossip columnists for decades.

Under normal circumstances Don Giovanni was played by a baritone, but Pinza was anything but normal. When in 1929 the manager of the New York Metropolitan, Giulio Gatti-Casazza, chose him to star in the house's first revival of the opera in 20 years, he was not only working against type, he was also threatening the stability of the house, since there were a good many baritones who believed themselves better qualified to sing the part. But Pinza's supreme stage presence, vivid characterization, and leonine voice won over even his most suspicious critics, and he established an ideal for the role that has never since been equaled.

The more Pinza played the Don, the more his private life appeared to mirror events on stage. Wherever he went in the United States, newspapers and journals delighted in reporting the course of his love affairs and his seemingly defining obsession with the opposite sex. After lunching with the singer in 1938, for example, the journalist Winthrop Sargeant wrote that "when Pinza is seated in a restaurant, the entrance of a good-looking girl will throw him into a trance-like condition like that of a well-bred hunting dog that has scented quail." Pinza was the target of million-dollar lawsuits from numerous women who felt that he had failed to make good on his "promises," and his lawyer was kept more than busy providing ludicrous excuses such as "It is Mr. Pinza's Italian background. Sometimes people think he is being romantic when he is just being gentlemanly."

Of course, there was more to Pinza than pheromones. His was one of the outstanding careers in Met history, spanning 22 seasons and some 51 roles. He was an actor of incomparable subtlety and versatility, adept at comedy, tragedy, and romance, and he was a model of vocal expression and technique.

He was also highly astute. In 1948, at the age of 56, when it was obvious his operatic career was nearing its end, he bowed out with one final Don Giovanni. He moved a few blocks from the Met to Broadway, and enjoyed a hugely successful career in musicals, operetta, and film, including a legendary run as the romantic hero in the first production of Rodgers' and Hammerstein's *South Pacific*.

Pinza earned for himself a reputation for womanizing. Crowds of screaming girls would gather outside the New York Met's stage door hoping to catch a glimpse of their handsome idol.

Lily
PONS
1898–1976

EVEN THOUGH SHE enjoyed a long and glittering career—more than a quarter of a century of which was spent at the New York Metropolitan—French, later American, soprano Lily Pons was never taken entirely seriously as an opera singer. For much of her career, and chiefly her time in New York, she was not unlike the fairy on a Christmas tree, in that she was perceived as something of an ornament, a weightless distraction from the substance of the tree rather than a part of the tree itself.

Despite more than 40 years on stage, Pons was never granted the respect that was hers by right. Her talent as one of the 20th century's greatest coloratura sopranos, and her influence as the progenitor of the bel canto revival of the 1950s and 1960s, has been largely discounted. Pons did not make her debut, in Mulhouse, France, as Lakmé (Delibes), until 1928, but after a brief period touring provincial opera houses, she was heard by the tenor Italian Giovanni Zenatello and his wife, Maria Gay, who recommended her to the manager of the Metropolitan, Giulio Gatti-Casazza.

Pons arrived in New York in 1931 at the height of the Depression, beneath which the Met was struggling to stay afloat. After hearing her rehearse, Gatti-Casazza decided to spring her on the city in a production of Donizetti's *Lucia di Lammermoor*. Leaked rumors whipped up a fair amount of interest, but nothing could have prepared the audience for the sensation produced by Pons' performance on January 3. Her singing was of unprecedented brilliance, and after the third act's "mad scene," the audience, it was reported, "applauded as if for their own lives."

Gatti-Casazza devoted himself to exploiting Pons' popularity, and she was alone in selling out every performance. As such, she effectively saved the Met from bankruptcy, for had she not appeared when she did, the opera house would have surely gone under. Pons knew her strengths and contained herself to a small repertoire of roles: Rosina (Rossini's *Il barbiere di Siviglia*), Amina (Bellini's *La sonnambula*), Gilda (Verdi's *Rigoletto*), Olympia (Offenbach's *Les contes d'Hoffmann*), Marie (Donizetti's *La fille du régiment*), and the title roles of *Lucia di Lammermoor* and *Lakmé*.

But the frothiness of this repertoire defined her standing in the eyes of the public, and she remained something of a lightweight during her time at the Met. This supposed inclination for trivia was confirmed during the 1930s when she appeared in three musical films—*I Dream Too Much* (1935) opposite Henry Fonda, *That Girl from Paris* (1936), and *Hitting a New High* (1937), the latter two opposite Lucille Ball. In fairness to Pons, however, her voice was miraculous, with an enormous range extending to a top F, and one of the greatest technical arsenals of the century. She was a superb performer and audiences, like Mr. Gatti, always walked away feeling as if they had got their money's worth.

The "darling of the songbirds," Pons was renowned for her exceptional coloratura in the operas of Donizetti, some of which—including La fille du régiment, *in which she is pictured here—were revived as vehicles for her talents.*

Rosa
PONSELLE

1897–1981

AFTER HEARING AMERICAN soprano Rosa Ponselle sing *La traviata* (Verdi) at the Met, Lotte Lehmann turned to Geraldine Farrar and asked: "How does one get a voice like that?" To which Farrar replied: "There's only one way: by a very special arrangement with the Lord—and then work, lots of work!" In truth, God had more of a hand in the evolution of what was probably the most perfect soprano in history than did sweat and tears. Although Ponselle studied voice during her youth, such was the completeness of her talent that she was able to give her first ever performance of an opera (as Leonora in Verdi's *La forza del destino*), at the tender age of 21, on the stage of the New York Metropolitan Opera alongside Enrico Caruso.

The first night created a sensation, leaving the audience reaching for its tissues and the critics for their adjectives. Ponselle was immediately recognized to be the perfect soprano: her voice was pure gold, with a dark, richly varied tone, a seamless legato, and flawless coloratura. The evenness of the tone and its projection, the elasticity of the vibrato, and the beauty of the phrasing were beyond measure, and had Ponselle wished to, she could have sung almost anything. Although she never performed Puccini or Wagner, this was probably as a dispensation to her colleagues, most of whom were sufficiently virtuous to acknowledge her comprehensive supremacy.

Ponselle remained at the Met, where she dominated her small but broadly pitched repertoire of 23 roles, for 19 seasons. Her most celebrated portrayal was Bellini's Norma, but she was no less triumphant in *Ernani* (Verdi), *Don Carlos* (Verdi), *La gioconda* (Ponchielli), *Andrea Chénier* (Giordano), *Guillaume Tell* (Rossini), *Cavalleria rusticana* (Mascagni), *La traviata* (Verdi), and *Don Giovanni* (Mozart). Ponselle generously supported a number of little-known contemporary operas, including Breil's *The Legend*, Romani's *Fedra*, and Montemezzi's *La notte di Zoraïma*. The only role in which she was thought less than ideal was Carmen (Bizet), produced in 1935. Ideally equipped though she was for the part, many thought her temperamentally unsuited to the character's fractured psychology, but for its part, the public was wholly seduced.

Ponselle retired from the stage two years later, aged 40, at the zenith of her powers. As privately made recordings demonstrate, her miraculous voice remained rich and flexible well into the 1950s, and it was one of opera's most keenly felt losses that she bowed out when she did. For those fortunate enough to have worked with her, there was no one greater. It was with unfeigned objectivity that Tullio Serafin, who during his 60-year career had conducted most of the greatest voices of the century, famously announced toward the end of his life that he had encountered only three true miracles of singing: Enrico Caruso, Titta Ruffo, and Rosa Ponselle.

The greatest of them all? Caruso and Serafin thought so. Ponselle's fairytale journey to the Met began during childhood, when her singing in a church choir led to performances with her sister in movie and vaudeville theaters.

Leontyne
PRICE

b. 1927

ALTHOUGH AS AN opera singer American soprano Leontyne Price was exceptional for the beauty of her voice, she was also the first African-American soprano not to see her race define the course and measure of her career. Unlike Marian Anderson and Grace Bumbry, both of whom struggled with prejudice, Price was treated as an equal from the outset and enjoyed, without fear of retribution or condemnation, the sort of latitude granted to her Caucasian colleagues. In her own way she did quite as much to further the cause of black emancipation in American musical life as her more politically animated predecessors. Price once remarked to an interviewer: "Marian had opened the door. I kept it from closing again."

It was Anderson who inspired Price to take up singing: "When I saw this wonderful woman come from the wings in this white satin dress, I knew instantly: one of these days, I'm going to be center stage, right there, where I saw her. I won't know what color the dress is going to be, but I'm going to be center stage." Soon after, Price won a scholarship to the Juilliard School of Music, where she made an emphatic impression, not least on the critic and composer Virgil Thomson, who in 1952 invited Price to make her debut as Saint Cecilia in a Broadway revival of his *Four Saints in Three Acts*.

Later that same year she scored a major success when she appeared as the heroine in Gershwin's *Porgy and Bess* in Dallas, Chicago, Pittsburgh, and Washington, D.C. The following year the production toured to London, Paris, Vienna, Berlin, Moscow, and, eventually, New York. The scene of Anderson's greatest triumph and the focus of Price's ambition, the New York Metropolitan, was apparently uninterested in her, even after an acclaimed appearance in a 1955 telecast as Tosca (Puccini) with the NBC Opera Theater. Subsequent telecasts of *Die Zauberflöte* (Mozart), *Les dialogues des Carmélites* (Poulenc), and *Don Giovanni* (Mozart) brought Price national celebrity but no invitation from New York. Instead, she was summoned to San Francisco, where she quickly became one of the city's best-loved stars. Further triumphs followed in Vienna, London, and Milan (all as Verdi's Aida) but still there came no invitation from New York.

Finally, on January 27, 1961, Price made her debut at the Met as Leonora (Verdi's *Il trovatore*) opposite another house virgin, Italian tenor Franco Corelli. It remains one of the most frenzied evenings in Met history, with each of the newcomers striving to outdo the other—to sensational effect, as a surviving recording testifies. But Price was the heroine of the hour, and from 1961 until her retirement in 1985, she was the darling of the New York opera scene. The voice was gloriously rich, with a burnished, almost husky tone that came into its own in the *lirico spinto* Verdi repertoire, particularly as the two Leonoras (*Il trovatore* and *La forza del destino*), Amelia (*Un ballo in maschera*), and Aida.

Price has done more to break down racial barriers in the world of opera than any other singer since Marian Anderson. Here she is pictured in role as Leonora (Verdi's Il trovatore*) in Salzburg in 1972.*

Samuel
RAMEY

b. 1942

AMERICAN BASS SAMUEL RAMEY is, in essence, the Plácido Domingo of the bass voice, in that he has managed to earn the respect of his critics and the affection of his audiences without compromising his obligations to either. The history of opera has seen many superstar sopranos, tenors, and baritones but few comparably revered basses. Many of the finest bass singers have been noted, first and foremost, for their acting skills. There have also been vocal gymnasts, gifted with voices of enormous range, power, and flexibility, while others have carved niches specializing in national and temporal areas of the repertoire. But only Ramey has succeeded in crossing the board internationally, as an actor and a singer, in such a diverse range of music.

Ramey's stature as an artist was apparent soon after his earliest performances at the New York City Opera (debut 1972) established him as a virtuoso of exceptional dexterity and invention. His dazzling technique was tailored uniquely to the coloratura demands of Rossini, Bellini, and Handel (as whose Argante in *Rinaldo* he made his sensational Met debut in 1984), as well as to the dramatic roles of Mozart and Verdi. During the early 1980s, it became apparent that he had a natural affinity for the French romantic repertoire, particularly the operas of Berlioz, Gounod, and Massenet. After adding the roles of Mefistofele (Boito) and Nick Shadow (Stravinsky's *The Rake's Progress*) to his repertoire, it became clear that Ramey was temperamentally suited to all things diabolical. As Mephistopheles in *Faust* (Gounod) and *La damnation de Faust* (Berlioz), he is without rival in modern times, and since he began playing all four villains in *Les contes d'Hoffmann* (Offenbach), he has monopolized all of the devil's best tunes.

In 1996 Ramey presented a sold-out concert at New York's Avery Fisher Hall titled "A Date with the Devil," in which he sang 14 arias representing the core of his repertoire. In 2000 he toured Europe and the United States with a series of "Date with the Devil" concerts. But despite the typecasting, Ramey's repertoire covers almost every aspect of the operatic canon—from Mustafà (Rossini's *L'italiana in Algeri*) and King Philip of Spain (Verdi's *Don Carlos*) to Boris Godounov (Mussorgsky) and Duke Bluebeard (Bartók's *Duke Bluebeard's Castle*). Aside from his collection of ensemble roles, he has done more than anyone to justify a revival of interest in some of the lesser-known areas of the bass repertoire, not least *Don Quichotte* (Massenet), *Attila* (Verdi), and *Maometto Secondo* (Rossini).

Aside from the operas of Wagner, Ramey continues to sing most of the major bass roles to outstanding effect. His glorious ringing voice and handsome stage presence have made him one of the world's most popular and bankable operatic stars—no mean feat for a bass. As one critic remarked after seeing Ramey as Boito's Mefistofele: "Any man that can make the bass repertoire appear sexy is probably not just pretending to be the devil."

Sporting an appropriately demoniac goatee beard in this photograph, it is easy to see why Ramey has earned a reputation for playing the Devil.

Mark
REYZEN

1 8 9 5 – 1 9 9 2

THE VOID CREATED by Fyodor Chaliapin's departure from Russia in 1921 was filled, almost immediately, by Russian bass Mark Osipovich Reyzen. For more than 60 of his 97 years, Reyzen was one of the heroes of the communist system, a People's Artist from 1937, and the single most creative influence on Russian bass singing after Chaliapin.

His popular and critical success as one of the finest singing actors of the 20th century was compounded at home by his devotion to the U.S.S.R. Indeed, aside from a protracted tour of Europe in 1930, when he performed in Berlin, Barcelona, Monaco, Paris, and London, Reyzen rarely left the country. Nonetheless, for most of his working life he was known by name and reputation throughout Europe and the United States as the dramatic *basso cantante* par excellence. If he was, by definition, a provincial rather than a global artist, then his small but outstanding body of recordings ensured that his impact on subsequent generations of singers has been as comprehensive as it has been widespread.

Reyzen turned to singing in his early twenties and made his debut in Kharkhov in 1921, as Pimen (Mussorgsky's *Boris Godounov*), progressing to Ruslan (Glinka's *Ruslan and Lyudmila*), Dosifei (Mussorgsky's *Khovanshchina*), the Miller (Dargomyzhsky's *Rusalka*), Basilio (Rossini's *Il barbiere di Siviglia*), Mephistopheles (Gounod's *Faust*), and Kotchubei (Tchaikovsky's *Mazeppa*). In 1925 he moved to Leningrad and in 1928 to Moscow and the Bolshoi, where he remained the star bass until 1954, when he retired to teach at the Gnesin Institute. He continued to perform, although rarely in public, and made records in his 80th and 87th years. In 1975 he gave a recital in celebration of his 80th birthday, and 10 years later, to general astonishment, it was announced that he would return to the Bolshoi in Moscow for a performance as Gremin (Tchaikovsky's *Eugene Onegin*).

Reyzen's achievements were vocal rather than professional, and his is now considered by many to be the most beautiful bass voice of the century. But it was the fluency of the delivery and the impeccable phrasing that set him apart from any of his colleagues. He was, in many respects, a tenor slacking as a baritone coasting as a bass—so broad was his technical mastery—and at a time when Russian basses were noted first and foremost for their profound depth and dramatic diction, rather than for their smoothness and elegance, Reyzen had it all. He was also an accomplished actor and a splendidly focused musician. His legacy of characterizations includes Boris (Mussorgsky's *Boris Godounov*), Salieri (Rimsky-Korsakov's *Mozart and Salieri*), Mephistopheles (Gounod's *Faust*), and Konchak (Borodin's *Prince Igor*), as well as the gamut of Wagner and Verdi. He is now a cult figure, whose recordings are of almost sacred value, and while he avoided the international spotlight during his lifetime, in death his reputation and legacy are becoming as widely appreciated as that of his revered predecessor, Chaliapin.

Reyzen was Fyodor Chaliapin's superior as a singer—his bass extended to an extraordinary two and a half octaves of tooth-rattling power and focus—and the only bass ever to rival him as an actor.

Titta
RUFFO

1877–1953

IN THE WORLD of opera, nicknames rarely provide an accurate caricature of their subject. One of the exceptions is Italian baritone Titta Ruffo, whose immense voice earned him the sobriquet "Voice of the Lion." The "Ruffo Roar" was without precedent, and it comes as no surprise to learn that, toward the end of Ruffo's life, the conductor Tullio Serafin pointed to him as one of the three miracles of singing—the other two being Enrico Caruso and Rosa Ponselle. Other singers had big voices, but Ruffo was in a class of his own, capable of producing a range, richness, and amplitude of tone that made him almost impossible to sing with and a nightmare to record.

Such was the scale of the voice, and so dramatic the artist wielding it, that only the most confident singers would agree to share a stage with him. When, in 1903, Covent Garden managed to raise the funds for him to appear in Britain, as Rigoletto (Verdi), his Gilda was none other than Nellie Melba. But when Melba heard Ruffo rehearsing, she quickly realized that her star was in the descendant, and under the pretext that (at 38!) Ruffo was too young for the role of the Jester, she had him replaced.

Ruffo appeared for the first time at La Scala, Milan, as Rigoletto during the 1903-04 season. Such was his success that he was assured an international career of extraordinary consistency and popularity. For the audiences at the Colón in Buenos Aires—where Ruffo performed regularly until the year of his retirement in 1931—he was almost a deity, while in the United States, where he first appeared in 1912 (in Philadelphia), he was generally thought to be without precedent or rival.

He was particularly feared by tenors, since the upper register of his voice reached so high and rang, according to English conductor Sir Thomas Beecham, like "the thrashing of a bell" that he would easily drown all but the most resonant voices. Not surprisingly, his favored partner was Caruso, who was his equal on every level. However, this unique equivalence gave their work together an air of the joust, and their few recordings *a due* stretched the technology of the time to its very limits. Their 1914 recording of the *Otello* (Verdi) duet "Sì, pel ciel" is the aural equivalent of watching two corpulent men cram themselves into a telephone box.

Ruffo's influence on the generation that followed him was enormous, and he can be credited with transforming the 19th century's polished, self-consciously gracious style of Italian baritone singing into the declamatory, forceful, often aggressive style that became common after the 1930s. There was more to Ruffo than muscle-flexing, however, for although largely unschooled, he was a famously hard-working autodidact. His character-izations were highly developed and well researched, reaching well beyond the one-dimensional formulas that informed the work of his predecessors.

With a voice of thunder and charisma dripping from every pore, Ruffo was the most respected (by his audience) and feared (by his rivals) baritone of his day.

Tito
SCHIPA
1 8 8 8 – 1 9 6 5

WHEN IN 1917 it was announced in New York that a young Italian tenor called Tito Schipa would be making his debut in a program of Neapolitan songs at the Town Hall, another Italian tenor, Enrico Caruso, asked for tickets. He had heard glowing reports of Schipa's talents and wanted to hear for himself what all the fuss was about. After the first few songs, Caruso quietly left the hall. When asked if he had not enjoyed Schipa's singing, Caruso replied: "Oh yes, he sings beautifully, but I have nothing to worry about."

It was a fair observation. Schipa was unquestionably one of the supreme talents of his day, a master stylist gifted with a voice of exquisite refinement, elegance, and expression. But as Caruso was relieved to discover, it was not a powerful voice and, as such, was wholly unsuited to the repertoire that Caruso had made his own. During the five years leading up to his first appearance at La Scala in 1915, Schipa had sung a broad range of music, including a number of *verismo* roles. However, from 1917, the year he created the role of Ruggero for Puccini in the first performance of *La rondine* in Monte Carlo, Schipa opted to specialize as a lyric tenor.

Unlike many of his lyric rivals, the tone of Schipa's voice was golden, with a husky quality that made it deliciously suggestive, and he carried it so well that it could fill even the largest theaters, including the New York Met, where he sang for three seasons between 1932 and 1935, and again in 1940. His repertoire was dominated by French romanticism, including *Lakmé* (Delibes), *Mignon* (Thomas), *Manon*, and *Werther* (both Massenet), and the lighter end of the bel canto spectrum, chiefly Nemorino (Donizetti's *L'elisir d'amore*), Ernesto (Donizetti's *Don Pasquale*), and Elvino (Bellini's *La sonnambula*).

He was uncomfortable with anything that required much above a B flat, and he never really had a high C, so that as the years passed, transposition became the rule rather than the exception. His popularity was founded not on pyrotechnics or melodrama but on phrasing. He was famous for being able to spin a line with more grace and style than any rival, Caruso included, and he could bewitch an audience through nothing more than the simplest diminuendo or shifted interval. He made a virtue of discipline and restraint, of grace and style, and even in later years, when he continued to perform into his seventies, he was never really limited by the gaps in his technique.

Schipa was first and foremost a stylist, which is not to say that his voice was anything other than beautiful to listen to, but in everything he did he was always thinking of the music and not the audience. His use of portamento and rubato are a model of taste and discretion, and serve to highlight the restraint and intelligence that defined his wonderful career. Schipa's longevity, and the unflagging vitality of his voice, may be attributed to a combination of patience, training, and innate modesty.

Schipa was a gentle, quietly spoken man with a voice of pure honey and gold. When he visited London for concerts after World War II, audiences thought it must be a different singer, so unchanged was his voice by time and use.

Elisabeth
SCHUMANN

1 8 8 8 – 1 9 5 2

CONSIDERING THE CULTURAL climate in which she made her name, and despite being on good terms with many of the greatest composers of the day, including Richard Strauss, it is extraordinary that German, later American, soprano Elisabeth Schumann should have achieved her legendary status without making a single contribution to the cause of contemporary opera. Indeed, she was the first internationally revered German soprano to thrive without recourse to the oxygen of contemporaneity. With the exception of Strauss's *Der Rosenkavalier*, the one modern (1911) opera with which she became widely associated, her reputation was founded entirely on revivalism. As such, she set the tone for postwar opera—that archival culture in which the leading singers have achieved their fame independent of the once-generic influence of the living composer.

Schumann was born in Merseburg, Germany, and studied in Dresden, Berlin, and Hamburg before joining the Hamburg Opera in 1909, where she remained for 10 years. In 1914 she made her New York debut at the Metropolitan Opera as Sophie in *Der Rosenkavalier*. Although Strauss's seduction occupied him for more than a year, he eventually managed to persuade Schumann to join the Staatsoper in Vienna, where he was joint director, in 1919.

Within a year of her arrival, Schumann became a staple of Viennese musical life—as a lieder recitalist as well as an opera singer—and it broke her heart when the Nazis' annexation of Austria compelled her to leave the city in 1938. Her friendship with Strauss was lifelong, although she never pretended to understand his collaboration with the Nazi administration. The two became especially close in 1921, when the composer invited her to join him on a lieder recital tour of the United States. Remarkably, he created no role for her glorious soprano, favoring instead the likes of Maria Jeritza, Lotte Lehmann, and Viorica Ursuleac, and he confined his affection for her talents to the composition of some of his most beautiful lieder.

Besides *Der Rosenkavalier* and the role of Sophie—which served as the vehicle for many of her house debuts, including her first appearance at Covent Garden in 1924—Schumann was commonly associated with the operas of Mozart, particularly the roles of Blonde (*Die Entführung aus dem Serail*), Susanna and Cherubino (both *Le nozze di Figaro*), and Zerlina (*Don Giovanni*). Her effortless, glowing voice was also revered as Eva in *Die Meistersinger* (Wagner), but she was not by nature a Wagnerian soprano. Indeed, so light was her voice that she was restricted to a relatively limited repertoire of roles. The voice was delicate but ringing and perfectly placed, with a crystalline purity that lent her performances—especially as Sophie—an air of perfection that, in the words of critic Peter Heyworth, "made singing sound as though it were the most natural thing in the world."

It was claimed that Richard Strauss's wife, Pauline, only allowed her husband to tour with Schumann because she did not perceive Schumann as a threat to her own highly subjective beauty.

Elisabeth
SCHWARZKOPF

b. 1915

WHAT DISTINGUISHES AN opera singer from a lieder singer when they are one and the same person? In the case of German soprano Elisabeth Schwarzkopf, very little. Thanks to her fanatical obsession with the primacy of the poet, she was one of the most controversial and fiercely debated singers of the 20th century, and in more ways than one she strove to represent the antithesis of the opera singer as songbird.

Schwarzkopf was, in this respect, the German Maria Callas. No two singers were ever more different vocally, but they shared a belief in the necessity for a character to live and breathe through their language, rather than on a floated cloud of song. Schwarzkopf began her career celebrated purely for the radiance of her voice, yet she, like Callas, ended it as one of the greatest vocal actresses of her generation.

Entering the Berlin Hochschule für Musik in 1934, Schwarzkopf began her studies as a mezzo-soprano, but within a year began retraining as a high soprano. Four years later she joined Berlin's Stätische Oper, where she made her professional stage debut as a Second Flower Maiden in Wagner's *Parsifal*. At conductor Karl Böhm's insistence, she left Berlin in 1946 to join the Theater an der Wien in Vienna, where she triumphed in a broad repertoire of roles. That same year she was invited to audition for Walter Legge, music director of EMI Records. Legge signed her to an exclusive contract, whereupon they began a close working relationship that led to marriage in 1953. Legge successfully remolded his wife into one of the most articulate lieder singers of the 20th century. Her flair for balancing the disparate needs of language and music inevitably colored her approach to opera, and although many criticized what they considered to be Schwarzkopf's artfulness and precious affectation, the results were often revelatory, not least on her many priceless recordings for EMI, such as Mozart's *Così fan tutte* (Karl Böhm, 1955).

In 1951 Schwarzkopf appeared as Anne Trulove in the world premiere of Stravinsky's *The Rake's Progress*, but she was otherwise no devotee of contemporary music. Indeed, from 1960 to 1967, she concentrated almost exclusively on five operatic roles: Donna Elvira (Mozart's *Don Giovanni*), the Countess (Mozart's *Le nozze di Figaro*), Fiordiligi (Mozart's *Così fan tutte*), Countess Madeleine (Richard Strauss's *Capriccio*), and the Marschallin (Strauss's *Der Rosenkavalier*), her most celebrated portrayal.

Schwarzkopf's voice had an exceptionally pure and transparent quality, and it is a testament to her integrity as an artist that she chose to reach beyond the undemanding confines of the bel canto for which she was naturally gifted. She worked toward an operatic symmetry that favored the restitution of a balance between the composer and the poet, for in the words of the Countess in *Capriccio*, "words and music are blended together to form a single creation. Mysterious experience—finding one art restored by the other."

While arguments still rage as to her qualities as an interpreter, no one disputes the essential beauty of Schwarzkopf's instrument—nowhere better demonstrated than in her performances as the Marschallin in Strauss's Der Rosenkavalier.

Beverly
SILLS

b. 1929

THE SOPRANO BEVERLY SILLS is something of an American legend. Even in her seventies, she is the embodiment of the dream that anyone, from anywhere, can do anything to which they set their mind. She was born in Brooklyn, New York, into relative poverty, and decided in her early teens that she wanted to be an opera singer. Her father was emphatically opposed to the idea since, according to Sills, "he thought only loose women went on the stage. When I asked him for his description of a loose woman, he said it was somebody who wore too much makeup, low-cut dresses, and changed the color of her hair."

Sills left home aged 15, supporting herself through performances with traveling theaters. Within six months Sills' father tracked her down in a production of *The Merry Widow* (Léhar). After the performance: "He stood there slowly looking me up and down. I then realized that the Merry Widow's dress was low cut (and I was a well-endowed 16-year-old), that I had bright red hair, and was wearing makeup with long false eyelashes. He said: 'You look terrible,' but after a brief pause he conceded, 'You sing like an angel. Come home and I'll pay for everything.' I was able to return home and study seriously." These studies enabled Sills to make her professional debut with the Philadelphia Civic Opera in 1947, as an 18-year-old Frasquita (Bizet's *Carmen*). After a number of years touring, she joined the New York City Opera in 1955 as the company's leading diva.

Sills' stature as an artist, and the extent of her vocal talent, was not fully recognized until 1966, when she sang the role of Cleopatra in Handel's *Giulio Cesare*. Almost overnight she was hailed as the finest American coloratura since Lily Pons, and the New York City Opera revived a series of bel canto operas especially for her. These triumphs led to invitations from Vienna in 1967, La Scala in 1969, Covent Garden in 1970, and the New York Metropolitan in 1975.

Sills could sing in Europe only during the summer vacation, when her children, two of whom were disabled, could travel with her. Her courage made her something of a heroine among American homemakers, and thanks to her many television appearances during the 1960s and 1970s, she became the popular embodiment of the opera singer. Unfortunately, she was never quite as good as her publicity. Sills lacked Maria Callas's dramatic weight, Joan Sutherland's technique, and Montserrat Caballé's tone, but she was a gutsy and committed performer who was capable of outstanding performances.

Her voice began to fail early in her career, and it was as something of a lifeline when Sills was invited to become director of the New York City Opera in 1979. As an administrator she rapidly stabilized the house's troubled finances. Artistically, she made the company a training ground for young talent, and the City Opera soon became known for its progressive repertoire and provocative stage work. Her father would have been proud.

Sills was the only American-born rival to the European bel canto virtuosos of the 1960s, and she was justifiably admired for her performances in the operas of Donizetti and Bellini.

Joan
SUTHERLAND

b. 1 9 2 6

ALTHOUGH MARIA CALLAS is widely considered to be the source of the bel canto revival of the 1950s, her contribution to the restoration of the romantic coloratura tradition pales beside that of Australian soprano Joan Sutherland. Sutherland's mastery of an essentially moribund style of singing and her revival of a wealth of neglected Italian and French operas represent one of the career landmarks in the history of 20th-century opera.

Many coloratura sopranos have followed in her wake, but none has so completely surmounted the technical and expressive demands of the florid style—a style of which Sutherland was largely ignorant until meeting her future husband, the conductor Richard Bonynge, at Covent Garden in 1952. With his support, and thanks to a period as a "soprano without portfolio"—in which she sang everything from *Aida* (Verdi) and *Die Zauberflöte* (Mozart) to Jenifer in the premiere of Tippett's *The Midsummer Marriage*—she was able to discover where her strengths lay as a soprano. These were famously highlighted in 1957, when she sang her first Gilda in *Rigoletto* (Verdi), but not until 1959, when she was given the title role in Franco Zeffirelli's production of *Lucia di Lammermoor* (Donizetti) at Covent Garden, was her talent as a dramatic coloratura fully realized.

Thereafter, Sutherland pursued an international career of extraordinary success and popularity, scoring legendary triumphs as Donna Anna (Mozart's *Don Giovanni*), Alcina (Handel), Lakmé (Delibes), Adina (Donizetti's *L'elisir d'amore*), Marie (Donizetti's *La fille du régiment*), and Violetta (Verdi's *La traviata*). But it was as a Bellini soprano that she achieved her greatest successes. Few of those fortunate enough to witness her performances as Beatrice (*Beatrice di Tenda*), Amina (*La sonnambula*), Norma, and Elvira (*I Puritani*) will forget the experience of having seen a soprano actually perform these roles as the composer intended.

Thanks to her invincible technique and rare musical intelligence, she could sing even the most difficult roles without giving the impression that they were in any way difficult. Consequently, she was able to inject traditionally empty characters with a warmth and human frailty that transformed the bel canto genre from an exercise in virtuosity into the gripping and emotionally sincere form of music theater imagined by Bellini and his peers.

Sutherland could skip through the highest passage work without breaking a sweat, but her diction was infamously poor. It would be fair to say, however, that no one went to hear Sutherland expecting to decipher even half of what she was singing. Ultimately, through her work in the theater and on her many recordings, Sutherland successfully fulfilled Bellini's maxim that his operas should drive "audiences to tears of emotion and ecstasy." She can be credited with having brought dignity and respect to a form of opera and a style of singing long disparaged by the operatic establishment.

Even in retirement, Sutherland's talents continue to throw a shadow over her successors, particularly in the role of Donizetti's Lucia (di Lammermoor), of which she is still thought to be the 20th century's undisputed master.

Francesco
TAMAGNO

1850–1905

FEW OF THOSE singers lucky enough to have been chosen by Verdi to create one of his leading roles survived to make recordings, and of those who did, only one, the Italian tenor Francesco Tamagno, can be heard in anything like his prime.

Tamagno was already a star when Verdi and his librettist, Boito, engaged him to create Gabriele Adorno in the premiere of the revised *Simon Boccanegra* in 1881. When, six years later, the same team was looking for a tenor to create the title role in its latest collaboration, *Otello*, Tamagno was still the leading dramatic tenor of the day and, for all his limitations, the obvious choice.

Unlike Iago, whom Verdi considered the province of a singing actor, the role of Otello necessitated a singer with a voice powerful enough to bring life to the character's violent emotional and mental collapse. In an ideal world Verdi would have preferred his tenor to have the skill to interpret as well as perform the role, but so demanding is its vocal range, and so combative the relationship between voice and orchestra, that Verdi had little choice but to opt for Tamagno's stentorian qualities.

As the first Otello, Tamagno created a perception of the role that has remained largely unchanged, and most of his successors (including Giovanni Zenatello, Mario del Monaco, Jon Vickers, Ramón Vinay, and Plácido Domingo) have opted for a declamatory and dramatic approach. With hindsight Tamagno can be seen as the first of that clamorous breed of tenor to culminate in the work of del Monaco and Franco Corelli.

Tamagno made his debut in 1870, as Nearco (Donizetti's *Poliuto*). Three years later he created a sensation as Riccardo (Verdi's *Un ballo in maschera)*. Thereafter he sang everything from Arnold (Rossini's *Guillaume Tell*), Edgardo (Donizetti's *Lucia di Lammermoor*), and Arturo (Bellini's *I Puritani*) to Don Carlos (Verdi), Radamès (Verdi's *Aida*), and Andrea Chénier (Giordano), specializing only insofar as he preferred singing in his mother tongue. Considering the size and power of his voice—which was compared by Amilcare Ponchielli to the striking of a bell—this complete lack of discretion strikes posterity as remarkable, not only because he was capable of navigating so many incongruous styles of singing but also because audiences didn't mind hearing arguably the loudest and least subtle tenor of the day hacking his way through the gems of the bel canto repertoire.

It is said that during the rehearsals for *Otello*, Verdi grew so exasperated with Tamagno's "free" approach to details of rhythm, meter, and pitch that he would drop the score and begin conducting the empty chairs of the stalls. To the Italian conductor Franco Faccio, he wrote of his hope that Tamagno might sing "something approximating to what I have written." In the event Tamagno so dominated the role that for many years after the first performances, cognoscenti refused to accept any other interpretation.

Tamagno is still something of a legend: a singer with the weight of voice and stamina required for Verdi's Otello *but who, nonetheless, built his reputation on the performance of bel canto.*

Richard
TAUBER

1 8 9 1 – 1 9 4 8

LONG BEFORE THE likes of the Three Tenors or Leslie Garett, the majority of early 20th-century opera stars made a virtue of what is now known as "crossover." Few, however, straddled the disparate worlds of serious and light opera as successfully as the Austrian tenor Richard Tauber. More than 50 years after his death, his name remains as synonymous with the operas of Mozart as with the operettas of Lehár, and it was thanks largely to his efforts that lighter music achieved a dignity long denied it by the snobbery of the European operatic establishment.

Tauber was born in Linz, Austria, the son of an actor and a soprano at the local theater. In 1913 his father secured him an engagement at the Dresden Opera, where for 12 years he reigned supreme as the company's leading lyric tenor. By the end of the 1920s, Tauber was one of the most popular musical figures in Germany and Austria, where he shone as the leading tenor at the Salzburg Mozart Festival. He began making records soon after his debut (completing a remarkable total of 735 78 rpm LPs), and from the outset, the warmth, vigor, and élan of the voice set him apart from any of his peers. The great size of the voice and his idiomatic Viennese style were not always suited to his choice of repertoire, but he was exactingly musical and he applied the same high standards to everything, no matter its composer or perceived audience.

His exactitude was particularly apparent during the 1920s, when he turned increasingly to lighter music, an interest that blossomed through a celebrated collaboration with the composer Lehár. This endured until the rise to influence of the Nazis, for even though Lehár was Hitler's preferred composer, there was sufficient Jewish blood in Tauber's veins to force him to leave for England. He carried his musical sympathies with him, and despite many invitations from Covent Garden, he made his British debut, in 1931, at Drury Lane in a new production of Lehár's *Das Land des Lächelns*. If Tauber had any concerns for his popularity outside Germany, these were quickly dispelled by his extraordinary success with the public, who so took him to their hearts that Tauber made England his permanent home.

While the popular end of the market idolized Tauber, many of his "serious" critics were contemptuous of what they perceived to be a waste of talent. Forcing his voice night after night did unquestionably weaken it. When he came to make his Covent Garden debut in 1938, he was no longer at his best, but he took the view that since there were enough great singers to keep the cognoscenti happy, the general public stood to gain the most from a comparable level of excellence. The chorus of disapproval was drowned out in 1947 when, with one lung collapsed from cancer, he sang Don Ottavio (Mozart's *Don Giovanni*) during a visit by the Vienna Staatsoper.

One of the best-loved singers of the 20th century, Tauber uniquely straddled the traditionally irreconcilable worlds of serious and popular music, achieving rare successes in tragedy as well as burlesque.

Renata
TEBALDI

b. 1922

WHENEVER ITALIAN OPERA fans gather to discuss their favorite soprano, they invariably concentrate on the technical quality of a voice, in isolation, rather than a singer's skills as an actress or dramatist. So when Italian opera fans try to agree on the most beautiful soprano voice of the 20th century, the singer most often cited is Italian Renata Tebaldi.

Lacking Maria Callas's intensity, and having little of the acrobatic dexterity common among her peers, Tebaldi compensated for her shortcomings with a voice of awe-inspiring beauty, the like of which has not been heard since her retirement in the 1970s. If her great rival Callas was the better actress, serving the poet before the composer, then Tebaldi had no need of a poet to hypnotize an audience. She was living proof of a belief in beauty for beauty's sake, and the absence of any legacy may be ascribed to the fact, emphasized frequently by critics, that her one defining achievement was actually God's.

After just four years of study, she made her debut in 1944, as Elena (Boito's *Mefistofele*), and in 1946 she auditioned for Italian conductor Arturo Toscanini, who was looking for a soprano to star in the reopening of La Scala. He was immediately seduced by the 24-year-old's extraordinary richness of tone, and despite her inexperience, he granted her the honor of singing at the opening night. From these far from humble beginnings was born Tebaldi's international career, and between 1949 and 1955, she was La Scala's leading lyric-dramatic soprano.

In 1950 she made her debut in London and San Francisco, and from 1954 she was a regular at the New York Metropolitan and the Chicago Lyric. Concurrently, she signed to record exclusively for Decca Records, for whom she made at least a dozen of the finest operatic recordings of the 20th century, famously as Mimi (Puccini's *La bohème*, 1951, 1958), Madama Butterfly (Puccini, 1951, 1958), Desdemona (Verdi's *Otello*, 1954, 1961), Violetta (Verdi's *La traviata*, 1954), and Madeleine (Giordano's *Andrea Chénier*, 1957).

For most of her admirers, Tebaldi's limitations were well-disguised strengths. In the age of Callas, there was a growing tendency to sacrifice the beauty of a voice on the altar of dramatic integrity. But for those who considered opera a fundamentally unrealistic art form, Tebaldi's luxurious voice reinforced the primacy of the composer and the music.

In later years Tebaldi's voice began to lose some of its fluency and the upper register began to take on water. With nothing else to rely on, it became plain to see that, as far as Tebaldi was concerned, beauty was all there was. She took the view that richness of tone precluded the need to resort to the ugly chest notes, piercing head tones, and ferocious vibrato common to a performance by Callas. In a perfect world, many would have liked to have seen Callas and Tebaldi share some of each other's qualities, but if most had to choose, the vote would go to Tebaldi.

A typically imperious pose from Tebaldi in a studio portrait from 1955, her last and, for many, her greatest year as part of the La Scala opera company in Milan.

Kiri
TE KANAWA

b. 1944

NEW ZEALAND SOPRANO Kiri Te Kanawa first made European headlines in 1971, after being picked from obscurity to sing the Countess in a new production of *Le nozze di Figaro* (Mozart) at Covent Garden. To most of those present at the first night, it was clear that the tradition of Mozart/Strauss sopranos embodied by Elisabeth Schumann, Lotte Lehmann, Elisabeth Schwarzkopf, and Lisa della Casa had found a new envoy in Te Kanawa. Her singing was remarkable for its freshness and vibrant tone, effortless placement, and instinctive phrasing, but it was the charm, maturity, and elegance of her stage presence that ensured her lasting success.

Thirty years on Te Kanawa continues to exercise an international appeal as one of the best-loved sopranos of the 21st century. For most people, however, she is the singer with the colorful hat and the nerves of steel who performed, before a television audience of a billion, Handel's "Let the Bright Seraphim" on July 29, 1981, at the wedding of Prince Charles and Lady Diana Windsor, while the happy couple were signing the register.

In the 10 years leading up to this celebrated event, Te Kanawa became the darling of the operatic world, scoring success after success in a small, but perfectly honed repertoire of roles. Aside from Mozart's Countess, she excelled as Donna Elvira (Mozart's *Don Giovanni*), Marguerite (Gounod's *Faust*), Micaëla (Bizet's *Carmen*), and Fiordiligi (Mozart's *Così fan tutte*). Her performances of the Italian repertory were less rewarding, for reasons that owed as much to temperament as to voice. Te Kanawa is a lyric, rather than a dramatic, soprano, and as Violetta (Verdi's *La traviata*), Amelia (Verdi's *Simon Boccanegra*), Mimi (Puccini's *La bohème*), Manon Lescaut (Puccini), and Tosca (Puccini), she has found neither the character nor the vocal weight necessary for a convincing portrayal.

There has been one notable exception to this rule: Desdemona (Verdi's *Otello*), the role with which she made her debut at the New York Metropolitan in 1974. She was called upon to cover for an indisposed Teresa Stratas just three hours before curtain-up, and her performance remains one of the most celebrated in the Metropolitan's history. No other soprano was so suited to the role of Otello's long-suffering wife, and Te Kanawa has practically owned Desdemona since the 1970s.

During the 1980s, when it was increasingly obvious that her talents lay outside the Italian arena, Te Kanawa turned—inevitably, some would say—to the lyric operas of Richard Strauss. As the Marschallin in *Der Rosenkavalier*, the title role in *Arabella*, and, from 1990, the Countess in *Capriccio*, she has exercised an influence comparable to that of her celebrated predecessors. If her approach to matters of style has been less individualistic than most, then this has generally been to the advantage of the operas, which breathe more easily when freed of the burden of heavy stylization.

Te Kanawa as the Marschallin (Strauss's Der Rosenkavalier*), a role to which—necessarily, perhaps—she came late in her career but one that she has eventually made her own.*

Bryn
TERFEL

b. 1965

FOR ALL THE fuss made about Wales being a nursery of great voices, few of them have found their way onto the stages of the world's leading opera houses. In recent years only one Welshman, the bass-baritone Bryn Terfel, has validated his country's reputation for vocal excellence. A solitary swallow though he is, it was never more the case that one true star is worth a dozen mediocrities.

Terfel was born with a voice of enormous natural potential that required discipline and technique, but little more. He was fortunate in being able to avoid the spotlight until two years short of his 30th birthday, when his performances and prizewinning at the 1993 Cardiff Singer of the World competition brought him to international attention. Sudden though his leap into the public eye was, Terfel had already been on the stage for three years, having made his debut as Guglielmo (Mozart's *Così fan tutte*) at the Welsh National Opera in 1990. He had also made recordings, including an acclaimed portrayal of Jokanaan in Strauss's *Salome*—a role he did not perform on stage until 1992, at the Salzburg Festival, where the critics fell over themselves reaching for superlatives.

The suddenness of Terfel's rise to prominence was breathtaking. Almost everyone pushed him to accept the dozens of offers that came rushing in after the Cardiff competition. Having sung the small role of Donner (Wagner's *Das Rheingold*) in 1993, he was widely informed that he was the finest Wagner bass-baritone since Hans Hotter, and requests for him to sing Wotan (Wagner's *Der Ring*) must have been very tempting.

With laudable resolve, however, Terfel resisted, and opted to carve for himself a career as a Mozartian, notably as Figaro and all three baritone roles in *Don Giovanni*. That he was ready for only some of what followed is undeniable, but it could have been a great deal worse. For the most part he survived the ravages of the blood-sucking music industry, rationing himself wisely in repertoire that he knew to be within his grasp. In recent years this prudence has paid generous dividends, and he has proven himself outstanding as Falstaff (Verdi), Nick Shadow (Stravinsky's *The Rake's Progress*), and Scarpia (Puccini's *Tosca*). But the constant pressure from his record company, Deutsche Grammophon, has resulted in some less than worthy products.

Terfel may well be one of the finest bass-baritones since World War II—with a voice of prodigious warmth and flexibility, and a dramatic flair second to none—but this in itself is not enough. Fortunately, he is also an intelligent and grounded individual, in complete control of his voice and career. Unlike those undeserving victims of the publicity machine, such as French tenor Roberto Alagna, Terfel promises to grow into a singer worthy of his public stature, and his brief career to date has proven that genuine talent can survive the parasite that is the contemporary business of opera and classical music.

A huge man with a commensurate voice, Terfel has built his reputation on larger-than-life characters, notably Jokanaan in Strauss's Salome *and the title role in Verdi's* Falstaff.

Luisa
TETRAZZINI

1 8 7 1 – 1 9 4 0

THE GENEROUSLY PROPORTIONED opera soprano has been a working cliché since the beginning of the 17th century. During the first quarter of the 20th century, when body fascism was still the preserve of those who could afford it, the queen of girth was Italian soprano Luisa Tetrazzini. A woman of leviathan proportions, she was blessed with a personality to match, and for much of her life she cared nothing for the comments of those who considered her appearance of greater interest than her singing.

The public's fascination with Tetrazzini's size, however, was a mere appendage to her fame. What made her famous in the first place was her voice, which counts among the five or six greatest of its sort in history. She was the coloratura soprano against which all others have since been measured. Her technical arsenal was more resourceful, and of greater refinement, than that of any of her contemporaries. She could sing almost anything, at any notice, and she made a virtue of the sort of acrobatic displays that have since been outlawed by what now passes for good taste.

It was a large, full-throated instrument that should not have been able to reach so high above the stave (to an easy E flat), or with such flexibility, but she did so consistently and without apparent effort. To German soprano Frieda Hempel, Tetrazzini claimed to have started life as a contralto. Not unsurprisingly, Hempel did not believe her, but after a brief demonstration, the astonished Hempel exclaimed, "Is there anything you cannot do?," to which Tetrazzini replied, "Well, Friedelina, some singers hava da figure, but Tetrazzini gotta da voice!"

The reaction to her first appearances in London, at Covent Garden in 1907, bordered on the hysterical, while in the United States she was so popular that she could command $2,500 a night—the equivalent of more than $100,000 today. On Christmas Eve, 1911, it was announced in Los Angeles that Tetrazzini would be giving an open-air concert outside the Chronicle Building. A quarter of a million people turned up, all of whom, it was claimed, could hear her perfectly clearly—without recourse to amplification. Her repertoire was dominated by bel canto, chiefly the roles of Violetta (Verdi's *La traviata*) and Gilda (Verdi's *Rigoletto*), but she was no less exceptional as Mathilde (Rossini's *Guillaume Tell*), Elvira (Bellini's *La sonnambula*), Marie (Donizetti's *La fille du régiment*), and Ophélie (Thomas's *Hamlet*).

Her voice never failed her, but nearly everyone she knew did. Having earned millions of dollars, she suffered from incompetent financial advice, outright theft, and a series of rakish husbands. A woman of immense charm, generosity, good humor, kindness, and talent, Tetrazzini was worthy of much better treatment. Her performances, on stage, in concert, and through her many recordings, brought pleasure to millions.

Toward the end of her life, friends would enquire after the health of Tetrazzini's voice. She would hit a high C on the piano, match it in full voice, laugh, and grandly announce: "I am old, I am fat, I am ugly—but I am still Tetrazzini."

Lawrence
TIBBETT

1 8 9 6 – 1 9 6 0

IN THE PANTHEON of great American singers, baritone Lawrence Tibbett went out of his way to convince the world that he was the greatest. Never was a singer so demonstrably pleased with himself, and while this air of the peacock can be explained by the genuine scale of his achievements—he was the first male American opera singer to secure international celebrity without first having earned his spurs in Europe—Tibbett's neon self-possession was the only obstacle to the fulfillment of his own expectations.

He was born in Bakersfield, California, to the sheriff of Kern County. When, in 1903, his father was shot dead by an outlaw, the family moved to Los Angeles. While still at high school, his musical ambitions began to take hold, and he gave numerous amateur performances around the county before coming to the attention of the poet Rupert Hughes, who sponsored his move to New York and a period of study with teacher Frank La Forge.

In 1922 he was engaged to replace Giuseppe de Luca as one of the Metropolitan's touring quartet (alongside Giovanni Martinelli), and the following year he joined the Metropolitan as a full-time company member. After a series of secondary roles, he was assigned Ford in a new production of Verdi's *Falstaff* in 1925, opposite Antonio Scotti. During the second-act monologue, the audience went berserk, standing for a 10-minute ovation, which was halted only after Tibbett agreed to take a bow. Thereafter, his stature as the leading American operatic baritone placed him on a par with the company's many European singers, and by 1930 he had eclipsed Scotti as the company's star baritone.

Although he sang with the Met for 27 seasons, taking part in numerous world premieres, as well as the first Met productions of *Simon Boccanegra* (Verdi), *Peter Grimes* (Britten), and *Jonny spielt auf* (Krenek), it was through his work in America's radio and film studios that Tibbett achieved his most popular successes. Although by no means conventionally handsome, his willingness to work with the slightest scripts and weakest directors made him a favorite with the studios, and through such forgettable classics as "The Cuban Love Song" and "The New Moon," he achieved a fame unprecedented among American singers. Indeed, by the end of the 1930s, his celebrity was such that when the gangster Bugsy Siegel decided to move to California, it was Tibbett's house on which he set his heart. Greeting him at the door, Siegel asked Tibbett what the house was worth and then offered twice the amount, in cash, so long as Tibbett left that afternoon. Ever the pragmatist, Tibbett took the money and left.

In 1940 a serious illness marked the beginning of the end of his once-glorious voice. In its prime he was capable of an extraordinarily subtle range of vocal nuance, from the lightest patter to the darkest thunder. But his self-assurance gave even his finest work a shallow ring, so that no matter how thick the makeup, the character was always Tibbett's.

A typically moody still of Tibbett from his film debut, The Rogue Story *(1930), which, though now lost, featured a cameo from comedians Laurel and Hardy.*

John
TOMLINSON

b . 1 9 4 6

EVEN IF ENGLISH bass-baritone John Tomlinson were not among the finest singing actors since World War II, his reputation would be assured simply by reason of his decade-long dominance of the bass-baritone repertoire at the Bayreuth Festival. That an Englishman should come to make such a vital contribution to this most German of institutions would have been unimaginable in 1971, when Tomlinson made his debut with Glyndebourne Touring Opera as Second Priest in *Die Zauberflöte* (Mozart). His teacher in London, Czech baritone Otakar Kraus, had performed at Bayreuth, but not even Kraus could have imagined that Tomlinson's enormous, dark voice would one day mutate into a bass-baritone capable of carrying off the arduous roles of Wotan (Wagner's *Der Ring*) and the Wanderer (Wagner's *Siegfried*), and then with such peerless authority and conviction.

For much of his first decade, Tomlinson was a bass, with a repertoire dominated by the work of classical and early romantic composers—chiefly Handel, Mozart, Rossini, Donizetti, and Verdi. Early in his career he also took an interest in modern music, and added the roles of King Fisher (Tippett's *The Midsummer Marriage*) and the Doctor (Birtwistle's *Punch and Judy*) to his repertoire. In 1991 he collaborated with Birtwistle on the first production of *Gawain*, in which Tomlinson created the role of the Green Knight. But by this stage in his career he had been singing for three years at Bayreuth, where he had established himself as the leading Wotan of his generation.

His current repertoire includes the Wagner roles of Hans Sachs (*Die Meistersinger*), Gurnemanz (*Parsifal*), Heinrich der Vogler (*Lohengrin*), and Hagen (*Götterdämmerung*), and Baron Ochs (Strauss's *Der Rosenkavalier*), Claggart (Britten's *Billy Budd*), Mephistopheles (Gounod's *Faust*), King Philip (Verdi's *Don Carlos*), and the title roles in *Le nozze di Figaro* (Mozart), *Boris Godounov* (Mussorgsky), and *Duke Bluebeard's Castle* (Bartók).

While his retraining for the extended reach and length of *Der Ring* resulted in some of the most impressive performances of Wagner since World War II, something was lost in the process. For all that Tomlinson has gained in range and power, there has been an equally marked loss of warmth and flexibility, and the magnificent declamatory quality for which he is so admired in Bayreuth has never fully compensated for the increasingly marked vibrato or the dilution of that glowing legato for which his earlier work was so remarkable.

OPPOSITE: As Wotan (Wagner's Der Ring*), Tomlinson is one of the few bass-baritones of recent years to truly fill the character's shoes.*

RIGHT: Tomlinson seeking to remove Gawain's head from his body as the Green Knight (Birtwistle's Sir Gawain and the Green Knight*).*

Richard
TUCKER

1 9 1 3 - 1 9 7 5

THE GOLDEN AGE of indigenous American opera singing that flowered during the 1950s and 1960s coincided with the ascendance of a small but influential coterie of Jewish singers, chief among whom was a quartet of male voices, the baritones Robert Merrill and Leonard Warren, and the tenors Jan Peerce and Richard Tucker. The latter was unusual in that he successfully reconciled his career as the most popular American-born tenor of the 20th century to his deeply held religious convictions—without compromising his responsibilities to either—and during his long and triumphant career, he came to epitomize the idealism, openness, and vitality of America's utopian dream.

Born in Brooklyn, New York, as Reuben Ticker, he began his career singing in synagogues, but did not make his stage debut until 1943, when he was engaged by the Salmaggi Company as Alfredo (Verdi's *La traviata*). In January 1945 he was snapped up by the director of New York Metropolitan, Rudolf Bing, to sing Enzo (Ponchielli's *La gioconda*). He remained the house tenor until his death exactly 30 years later.

At the beginning of his career, Tucker specialized as a *lirico spinto* tenor, with notable successes in middle-period Verdi and early Puccini. In his late thirties, however, Tucker's voice darkened and grew in both weight and stamina, so that he was able to shift up a gear and tackle the dramatic Italian repertoire, including Manrico (Verdi's *Il trovatore*), Canio (Leoncavallo's *Pagliacci*), Radamès (Verdi's *Aida*), and Alvaro (Verdi's *La forza del destino*). In the latter he was unrivaled, demonstrating an extraordinary vocal power and energy that for New Yorkers presaged the melodramatics of Franco Corelli by nearly a decade.

Indeed, Tucker was something of a phenomenon in that, despite his New York Jewish upbringing, he was among the most Italianate tenors of his day. Prior to Corelli's arrival in 1961, only Giovanni Martinelli and Beniamino Gigli could match Tucker for sobbing, yelping, and swooping. Although his fostering of Italianate affectation could have easily come across as misjudged, so committed were his performances, and so virulently energetic was his singing, that audiences would have been forgiven for thinking him as Italian as pasta—even if his pronunciation was as Italian as pizza.

Inevitably, perhaps, the muscle-flexing came at a cost. Tucker's performances were often at the high end of exciting, but they were rarely subtle, complex, or refined. He was not a big man, and he compensated for his lack of physical presence through committing every fiber of his being to every performance. Consequently, there was often little to distinguish his Rodolfo (Puccini's *La bohème*) from his Alvaro (Verdi's *La forza del destino*). Only at the very end of his career, when in 1973 he finally achieved his lifetime ambition of performing Eléazer in Halévy's *La juive*, did he reach sufficiently deeply into a characterization for his singing to count for less than his portrayal.

Tucker was blessed with a hugely energetic and virile voice, but he was less animated as an actor. This studio portrait of the tenor as Cavaradossi (Puccini's Tosca*) gives some idea of his thespian range.*

Eva
TURNER

1892–1990

THE CONTRIBUTION MADE by English singers to the history of 20th-century opera has been slight, to say the least. Of the five English names in this book, one performed only two operas, another devoted himself to the work of a single composer, while a third spent almost his entire career in Vienna. Except for John Tomlinson, only one English singer, soprano Eva Turner, enjoyed a reputation on the Continent equivalent to her standing at home, where she was revered as one the finest dramatic sopranos of the 20th century.

Turner was born in Oldham, Lancashire, an area not traditionally associated with the cultivation of great opera singers. In her 10th year her family moved to Bristol, where Eva was taken to a performance of *Il trovatore* (Verdi) by the Carl Rosa Opera Company. Before the end of the first act, she had determined to become an opera singer. Thirteen years later, toward the end of a four-year course at the Royal College of Music, she auditioned for the company that had inspired her and was engaged as a chorus member.

In 1916 she made her solo debut, as a Page in *Tannhäuser* (Wagner), following which she remained with the company for eight years, singing a huge range of music that embraced everything from Donna Anna (Mozart's *Don Giovanni*) and Marguerite (Gounod's *Faust*) to Tosca (Puccini) and Brünnhilde (Wagner's *Der Ring*). In 1924 a chance encounter with the Argentinean conductor Ettore Panizza changed her life forever. He heard her perform Madama Butterfly (Puccini) at the Scala Theatre in Charlotte Street, realized that she was better suited to that other Scala, in Milan, and arranged for her to audition for the music director, Arturo Toscanini. Toscanini immediately offered Turner the Wagner roles of Freia in *Das Rheingold* and Sieglinde in *Die Walküre*.

Thereafter, Turner's career was assured, and for the next 20 years she toured Europe to glowing acclaim, specializing in Aida (Verdi), Leonora (Verdi's *Il trovatore*), and, from 1926, Turandot (Puccini). As the icy princess, Turner was miraculous. According to Franco Alfano, who completed the score after Puccini's death in 1924, Turner was the ideal, vocally and dramatically, which was a truer verdict than he probably realized.

Indeed, Turner was a very distant performer, vocally precise and dramatically calculated, and while these were generally considered to be mandatory qualities for Turandot, they were less suited to the remainder of her repertoire. Audiences may have been united in their admiration for Turner's voice, but there was always division when it came to her core repertoire of Verdi and Wagner. For all her globetrotting, her most devoted fans were in London. Her finest hour came in 1937, when she sang Turandot to Giovanni Martinelli's Calaf in performances that many feel have never been bettered. Certainly, the surviving recordings testify to a portrayal of an erotic intensity for which audiences were palpably unprepared. After all, Turner was from Oldham

It is doubtful that Turner approved of this studio portrait of her dressed to kill as Turandot (Puccini), but the intensity of the stare hints at the concentration of her performances.

Astrid
VÁRNAY

b. 1918

THE RISE TO fame and glory of the Swedish, later American, dramatic soprano Astrid Várnay is a very modern example of necessity smothering discretion. The postwar shortage of big-voiced sopranos created a situation in which singers who, 30 years earlier, would probably not have progressed to the first rank found themselves pushed to the footlights of the world's leading opera stages for want of anything better. Astrid Várnay is a case in point. Unquestionably gifted as an actress, Várnay nonetheless possessed a voice that was born unattractive and matured into something downright ugly. This is not to suggest that she was unworthy of her career as one of the leading Wagner sopranos of her generation. It merely emphasizes the need for compromise that characterized Wagner production in Germany upon the reopening after World War II of the Bayreuth theater in 1951.

In 1920 Várnay's family emigrated to the United States, where she studied singing with her mother, the coloratura soprano Maria Yavor, and later the Wagner coach Hermann Weigert, whom she went on to marry. Unlike most of her predecessors, Várnay underwent no apprenticeship. She did not work her way through the lighter end of the repertoire in provincial theaters, and she made no study of the voice in a manner that the prewar generation might have recognized. Instead, a last-minute withdrawal by Lotte Lehmann led Várnay to make her debut at the New York Metropolitan Opera as Sieglinde (Wagner's *Die Walküre*) on December 6, 1941, at the grand age of 23. The following afternoon the Japanese launched an air attack on Pearl Harbor, which put paid to any glowing press coverage.

In 1948 Várnay made her European debut at Covent Garden. Three years later she was invited by Wieland Wagner to Bayreuth, on the recommendation of Norwegian soprano Kirsten Flagstad—for the only time in the theater's history, without an audition—where she sang Brünnhilde in two *Ring* cycles.

Varnáy's intensely dramatic but vocally suspect performances may not have been to everyone's tastes, but she could dominate a scene through the sheer concentration and vehemence of her personality. After 30 years singing the heaviest, most dramatic roles in the repertoire, Várnay built a successful second career playing character parts, such as Herodias (Richard Strauss's *Salome*) and Klytemnästra (Strauss's *Elektra*). The physical began to play an even greater hand in her work, but this time her aggressive and declamatory vocal complexion worked to her advantage, and as the maternal figures in *Salome* and *Elektra* she was capable of shocking even the most uninterested opera-goers. Várnay's voice was a torn and bloody affair, in which wobbling and screaming played a greater part than was absolutely necessary, but she was utterly captivating on stage.

Várnay shot to fame at a time when her talents as a Heldensopran *were in conspicuously short supply, and although many now wince at her lack of vocal delicacy, few would contest her range and amplitude as a singing actress.*

163

Jon
VICKERS

b. 1926

THE DEVELOPMENT OF recording has nowhere been more damaging than in its impact on the public expectation of its tenors, and in particular the *Heldentenor* (a robust tenor suited to dramatic roles). Before the advent of the gramophone, reputations were founded on hearsay, the written word, and individual prejudice. Had the Canadian tenor Jon Vickers been born a century earlier, history would have had nothing more dependable on which to base its judgment than nostalgia, and fresh talents could have emerged free of the suffocating burden of precedence. But Vickers' vocal maturity coincided with that of the gramophone and, as such, he has cast a terrible shadow over subsequent *Heldentenors*.

On stage Vickers was a force of nature, with a compelling bearing to match his electrifying, if unorthodox voice. He used little head resonance, and thus lacked ringing high notes; he suffered from an unsteadiness that frequently degenerated into a wobble; he struggled with anything high above the stave, and he was forced to resort to falsetto when singing quietly. However, he was a uniquely forceful performer—so much so that many of his stage partners found him almost too intense. Whenever American baritone Sherrill Milnes sang Iago to Vickers' Otello (Verdi's *Otello*), Milnes would tone down his portrayal for fear that the tenor might throw him bodily off the stage, so involved did Vickers become with the character he was playing.

Presaged only by Chilean tenor Ramón Vinay, Vickers specialized in the heavyweight dramatic repertoire, which embraced everything from Berlioz's Aeneas (*Les Troyens*) and Verdi's Otello to Wagner's Tristan (*Tristan und Isolde*) and most of the *verismo* repertoire. Unlike Vinay, however, he was able to modify the scale of his voice to encompass other, less vocally demanding roles—notably Jason (Cherubini's *Médée*) and Florestan (Beethoven's *Fidelio*), among others. He was particularly revered by the conductor Herbert von Karajan, who made him a fixture of the Salzburg Festival. He made a meteoric impact at Bayreuth, where he first appeared in 1958 as Siegmund (Wagner's *Die Walküre*). Tragically, differences of opinion and clashes of personality prevented the relationship with Bayreuth from developing as might have been expected, and he subsequently gave most of his finest Wagner performances in Vienna and New York.

Vickers was an uncommonly vehement performer and, consequently, not the easiest man to work with. Many of his more unorthodox attitudes were informed by his allegiance to Christian Scientology, thanks to which he would analyze the character of each of his roles to the extent that he began to hate some of them—as he famously did Tristan (Wagner's *Tristan und Isolde*). His beliefs also led him to some curious career decisions, perhaps the most notorious of which was his withdrawal in the 1970s from a Covent Garden production of Wagner's *Tannhäuser* on "religious grounds."

One of the giants of the operatic stage, Vickers was a humbling presence, projecting an uncommon strength of character and conviction with a voice of gargantuan proportions.

Ramón
VINAY
1912–1996

WHILE A NUMBER of the 20th century's most celebrated dramatic tenors were noted for the clamor of their singing, most of them proved that shouting was no substitute for passion, and that eye-rolling and face-pulling were, in themselves, no more than an artificial gesture toward a reflective characterization. The singer who, more than any other, demonstrated this time and time again, with neither precedent nor equal, was the Chilean tenor and baritone Ramón Vinay.

Where his contemporaries sang the role of Verdi's Otello, often extremely well, Vinay became the character, and he would seduce an audience into believing in him, his tragedy, and his downfall. Vinay was a performer of such elemental power and emotional authority that, as Otello, his submission to even the most ludicrous of Iago's subterfuges carried within it the gravity of inevitability. The scale of the voice defied analysis, so huge was the instrument, but it was the astounding power and magnetism of the man that animated what would otherwise have been little more than yet another operatic matador in tights painting human frailty by numbers.

Like many of the 20th century's more dramatic tenors, Vinay began his career as a baritone, making his debut as Alfonso (Donizetti's *La favorite*) in 1931. Twelve years later, after intensive vocal studies with the tenor René Maison, he made his debut as a tenor, singing Don José (Bizet's *Carmen*). In 1944, shortly before his 32nd birthday, he sang his first Otello, and the following year he made his debut at the New York Met, remaining a fixture at the house until 1961.

His international career took off in 1946 when the conductor Arturo Toscanini invited him to sing Otello for his recording of the opera, and in 1951 he repeated the role for conductor Wilhelm Furtwängler at the Salzburg Festival. The following year he appeared for the first time at Bayreuth, after which he devoted himself almost exclusively to Wagner. In 1962 Vinay returned to the baritone repertoire, making his last appearance as Iago (Verdi's *Otello*) at the Opera of Santiago de Chile in 1969.

Bayreuth's musical director Wieland Wagner described Vinay as "the eighth wonder of the world," while conductor Karl Böhm claimed him the "raging incarnation of obsession." He made only one studio recording, of Verdi's *Otello* (Toscanini, 1947), but his many live recordings admirably capture him in full flow. His voice was a kaleidoscope of human emotion. It was far from beautiful, and as the years passed, so the vibrato widened and the tone roughened. But Vinay was capable of a broader range of feeling than any other tenor of the century—from an almost childlike fragility to an animal ferocity of terrifying proportions. For those who followed him, Vinay's artistry has represented the ideal, while at the same time creating a precedent that will probably never be surpassed.

Vinay was one of the most complete singing actors of the 20th century, blessed with a voice of fearsome power and intensity. He is seen here as Samson (Saint-Saëns' Samson et Dalila), one of his handful of tenor roles.

Leonard
WARREN
1911–1960

LIKE FRANCO CORELLI and Renata Tebaldi, the American baritone Leonard Warren was a singer whose voice removed him from the normal critical universe in which everyone else worked. As "a voice" he was almost entirely without skill as an actor, and relied on the stock gestures of the 19th-century operatic ham to get him through a portrayal. No one cared. In fact, very few among his audiences ever noticed, because he was born with the sort of jaw-dropping voice that was its own distraction.

Warren's voice was an instrument of fantastic range and power that extended all the way to a tenor's high C. Aside from its scale, the voice was gloriously warm and rich, with an easy projection and seductive legato, but it was also capable of inflamed drama, with a roar that brought about fully warranted comparisons with his only real predecessor, Italian baritone Titta Ruffo.

Warren was born Leonard Warenoff in New York into a family of second-generation Russian Jewish immigrants. It was not until 1935, when he entered the choir of the Radio City Music Hall in New York, that his talent was discovered. Warren progressed to private studies in New York and Milan, and in 1938, with a repertoire of just five operatic arias and a small selection from Verdi's *Rigoletto*, he won the New York Metropolitan Opera Auditions. On November 27, 1938, Warren made his debut, at the Metropolitan, in excerpts from *La traviata* (Verdi) and *Pagliacci* (Leoncavallo). At the time he had seen only one complete opera performance. Not since Rosa Ponselle's heady ascension to the Met's footlights in 1918 had a singer progressed so far with so little experience. But the risk paid off, and less than six months after his debut, he was given his first complete role, as Paolo (Verdi's *Simon Boccanegra*).

Thereafter, he reigned supreme as the Met's leading baritone, particularly in the operas of Verdi. Among his preferred characters were his signature role as Rigoletto, of which he gave 88 performances at the Met, and his Macbeth, Conte di Luna (*Il trovatore*), Germont (*La traviata*), Don Carlo (*La forza del destino*), and Iago (*Otello*). Warren's dedication to perfection was legendary. He eschewed the fizzing social life enjoyed by many of his colleagues for a life of hard work, as reflected in the more than 600 performances he gave at the Met between 1939 and his death in 1960, aged 48.

Warren died midway through a performance of *La forza del destino*. Having sung the words "O joy, O joy," he fell to the ground, having suffered a massive heart attack, and was pronounced dead 20 minutes later. The horrified audience waited in silence until the manager of the Met, Rudolf Bing, came in front of the curtain and announced: "This is one of the saddest nights in the history of the Metropolitan." As gasps of "No" rose from the audience, Bing asked the theater to rise "in memory of one our greatest performers."

Warren rarely made anything more than a cursory attempt to act out a role. He didn't need to, particularly as the jester Rigoletto in Verdi's opera of the same name.

Wolfgang
WINDGASSEN

1914–1974

IT IS A MEASURE of how grim the current situation in opera is that the career of German *Heldentenor* Wolfgang Windgassen is now looked upon with nostalgic reverence. For much of his life, he was subjected to almost uninterrupted criticism—the major part of which asserted that he was not, in fact, a *Heldentenor* at all.

In his memoirs the producer Wolfgang Wagner claims that, in 1950, during one of their recruitment drives for Bayreuth, he and his brother Wieland drove to Munich to hear a performance of Wagner's *Die Meistersinger* conducted by Hans Knappertsbusch. The role of Walter was being sung by Windgassen, then known primarily as the son of Fritz, who had been the leading tenor at Stuttgart Opera from 1923 to 1944. When the Wagners greeted Knappertsbusch in his dressing-room, the conductor announced: "Gentlemen, I hope you don't take it into your heads to engage that *Krawattltenor* [a tenor whose tie is more impressive than his voice]." Wolfgang thought it best not to mention that they had already approached Windgassen with a view to signing him for the next year's production of Wagner's *Parsifal*—to be conducted by one Hans Knappertsbusch.

As things turned out, the conductor's fears were unfounded since Windgassen proved more than capable of filling Parsifal's shoes, and, despite fundamental weaknesses, he later matured into one of the most consistent *Heldentenors* of his generation. That his generation produced no more than half-a-dozen tenors capable of performing the Wagner repertoire puts his dominance into some sort of perspective, but even if there had been a glut of talent, Windgassen's status would still be assured.

He proved that the *Heldentenor* does not, as a prerequisite, have to make a lot of noise. Although the prewar stars Max Lorenz, Franz Völker, and Lauritz Melchior were gifted with big voices, the scale and richness of their basic tone mattered less than the consistency, clarity, and evenness of their performances. Richard Wagner wanted every word to be understood. He also wanted his singers to persevere to the end of a performance, and what Windgassen lacked in vocal weight, he compensated for with stamina. Moreover, he was a singer of instinctive musicality, and he brought a studied discernment to his work that was rare among his predecessors and almost extinct among his contemporaries.

During the 1950s and 1960s, Windgassen was an annual fixture of the Bayreuth Festival and sang Siegfried on the three most important recordings of the *Ring* cycle—conducted by Krauss (1953), Solti (1958–1965), and Böhm (1966–1967). But he lacked animal excitement, and this was a quality valued above almost any other by audiences for whom the prewar generation had defined the mold. Yet Windgassen remains one of the true heroes of Wagner singing—an artist who through the careful marshaling of his resources was able to dominate a repertoire for which he was fundamentally unequipped.

Unintentionally, no doubt, Windgassen spent most of the 1960s, when he was the leading tenor at the Bayreuth Festival, made up to look like Liberace. He was no less entertaining as a performer.

Fritz
WUNDERLICH

1930–1966

TWENTIETH-CENTURY OPERA has witnessed few tragedies more keenly felt than the death of German tenor Fritz Wunderlich shortly before his 36th birthday. No other singer of his generation warranted such unqualified respect and affection from audiences, colleagues and critics, and no other carried the burden of so many people's hopes and expectations. At his death, Wunderlich was the world's leading German lyric tenor, and among the most perfect singers of the 20th century.

He was gifted beyond measure with a voice of absolute flawlessness, as smooth in its placement, warm in its tone, and free in its delivery as could be imagined. Indeed, it was often said of his performances that they normalized perfection, and few would argue that since his death there has been no tenor, German or otherwise, to come close to Wunderlich in his preferred repertoire.

His repertoire was dominated throughout his career by Mozart, as whose Tamino (*Die Zauberflöte*) Wunderlich sang at his 1955 debut at the Freiburg Musikhochschule, where he studied singing and the French horn from 1950 to 1955. His appearance in this student production led to a contract at the Württemberg State Opera in Stuttgart, where he made his professional debut as Ulrich Eislinger in Wagner's *Die Meistersinger*.

When, after six months of supporting roles, he was called to play Tamino instead of an ailing Josef Traxel, Wunderlich was catapulted to fame—and his pick of the repertoire, which rapidly grew to embrace everything from Haydn, Handel, and Beethoven to his beloved operettas, of which he was absolute master. However, one of Wunderlich's maxims was "the vocal cords are not fists" and that "to the age of 35 a voice needs nursing." He was, therefore, careful not to accept any engagement that might in some way have damaged his voice. Yet for all his caution, Wunderlich's repertoire was bewilderingly expansive—he sang 55 roles in his short career.

In 1958 he joined the Frankfurt Opera, and in 1959 he appeared for the first time in Salzburg. Thereafter, he was one of the brightest stars in the operatic firmament, giving now-legendary performances in Vienna, Dresden, and Munich. He was exceptionally gifted in the music of Richard Strauss, and his performance as Leukippos in a 1964 production of *Daphne* conducted by Karl Böhm is one of the miracles of the age.

It was a voice of spellbinding virility, energy, richness, and beauty, and many people prayed that he would turn to the Wagner repertoire for which his voice was the ideal. But it was never to be. On September 17, 1966, Wunderlich fell down a stone stairway in Heidelberg and fatally fractured his skull. Although he never realized his full potential, his legacy is fantastically rich, and for all that he left unfinished, there are enough recordings to remind us of the achievements for which his glorious career is so remarkable.

Very probably the most perfect German lyric tenor of all time, Wunderlich possessed a voice of unique smoothness, sweetness, and warmth, and much the same could be said of his personality, which endeared to him to everyone.

Giovanni
ZENATELLO
1876–1949

AT THE END of the 19th century, the Italian tenor voice was, for the most part, a light-weight instrument. But by 1900 the new, dramatically intense style of opera had begun to influence the tone and weight of operatic voices, particularly tenors, and the first tenor to become synonymous with this radical new approach was Italian Giovanni Zenatello.

Zenatello began his career as a baritone, making his debut in 1898 as Silvio (Leoncavallo's *Pagliacci*). When, the following year, he made his tenor debut as Canio in the same opera, he was an overnight sensation. Audiences were overwhelmed not only by the power and emphasis of his singing but also by his articulate, highly expressive enunciation, which was wholly unlike anything then in circulation.

In 1902 Zenatello was engaged by the conductor Arturo Toscanini at La Scala for performances in Berlioz's *La damnation de Faust* and Verdi's *Un ballo in maschera*. These brought him to the attention of the composers Giordano, who chose him for the first performance in 1903 of *Siberia*, and Puccini, who, in 1904, invited Zenatello to create the role of Pinkerton in the premiere of *Madama Butterfly*. Although the opera was initially a failure, Zenatello's part in it was widely praised, and he returned to the role when the composer's three-act revision of the score was wheeled out three months later.

Thereafter, Zenatello toured the globe as one of the first tenor superstars. He was a huge celebrity in Buenos Aires between 1903 and 1910, and he made regular appearances at Covent Garden between 1905 and 1926. But from 1907, when he made his New York debut at Oscar Hammerstein's Manhattan Opera Company, Zenatello spent most of his time in the United States. Somewhat overshadowed by the Enrico Caruso phenomenon, he was nonetheless hugely popular, particularly in that small area of dramatic repertoire neglected by Caruso—chiefly the title role in Verdi's *Otello*.

As recordings from the 1920s amply demonstrate, Zenatello was a magnificent, imperious Moor, and his baritonal timbre, rich coloring, and bell-like upper register gave him an authority in the role that was challenged only by Chilean Renato Zanelli and (on a very good day) compatriot Giovanni Martinelli. Zenatello made no virtue of vocal beauty and, as an instrument, his tenor was very much of its time, inclining toward a coarseness that preempted the gladiatorial vulgarities of Italian Mario del Monaco. But he was an exciting performer, and in his core repertoire, this was a quality valued above any other.

He retired in 1928 and returned to Italy in the 1930s, where he took up the management of the Verona Arena, which he had inaugurated in 1913 as Radamès (Verdi's *Aida*). One of his last triumphs, in 1947, was his supervision of the Veronese debut of a young Greek-American soprano called Maria Kalogeropoulou who, for her appearance as La gioconda (Ponchielli), was persuaded to change her name to the more pronounceable Callas.

It is unfortunate that very few "action" photographs of singers survive from the early 20th century. Zenatello, for one, cut a sensational figure on stage—a reputation to which this formal portrait contributes little.

Index